CW00557319

DIDCOT TO BANBURY

Vic Mitchell and Keith Smith

Cover picture: No. 6136 runs north through Radley, the junction for Abingdon, sometime in the early 1960s. By the end of that decade, vast tonnages of coal would be transported on the route with the opening of Didcot Power Station. (M.J.Stretton coll.)

Published February 2003

ISBN 1 904474 02 0

Design Deborah Esher
David Pede
Typesetting Barbara Mitchell

Published by
Middleton Press
Easebourne Lane
Midhurst, West Sussex
GU29 9AZ
Tel: 01730 813169
Fax: 01730 812601

Printed & bound by Biddles Ltd,
Guildford and Kings Lynn

CONTENTS

ACKNOWLEDGEMENTS

Our sincere gratitude goes to so many of the photographers who have helped us and also to W.R.Burton, H.Cowan, L.Crosier, G.Croughton, G.Heathcliffe, N.Langridge, J.S.Petley, Mr D. and Dr S.Salter, N.W.Sprinks, C.Stacey, E.Youldon and, as always, our wives.

I. GWR map of 1910 (GWR Magazine)

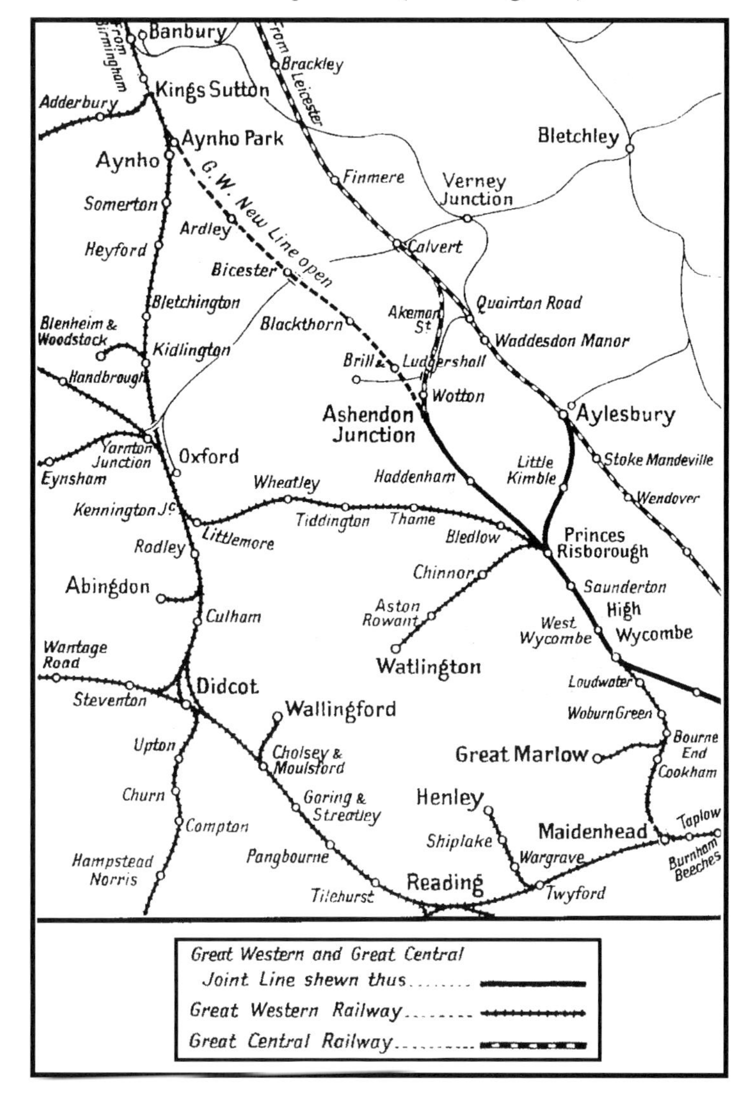

GEOGRAPHICAL SETTING

The line follows the Thames Valley from Didcot to Oxford, although, due to a meander, it is remote from the river in the vicinity of Culham. However, the Abingdon branch was close to the Thames, that town also being on a meander.

From Oxford to Banbury, the railway is close to both the River Cherwell and the Oxford Canal. The route is on a gentle up gradient, climbing from 200ft above sea level at Didcot to 300ft at Banbury. The branch to the small town of Woodstock climbed slightly from the floor of the Cherwell Valley, near Hampton Gay.

The underlying geology is varied. The route starts on an outcrop of Upper Greensand and is on Kimmeridge Clay in the vicinity of the Abingdon branch. An extensive outcrop of Oxford Clay surrounds the ancient university from which it takes its name.

North of Kidlington, the main line and much of the branch to Woodstock is on Oolitic Limestone of value particularly for cement production. The route continues to the market town of Banbury on a mixture of Clay and Limestone forming the northern extension of the Cotswolds.

Most of our journey is in Oxfordshire, but a section in the Aynho-Kings Sutton area is just in Northamptonshire. The southern part used to be in Berkshire, as did Abingdon.

The maps are at the scale of 25ins to 1 mile, unless indicated otherwise. North is at the top, except where there is an arrow.

II. Gradient profile with mileage chart on the lower border.

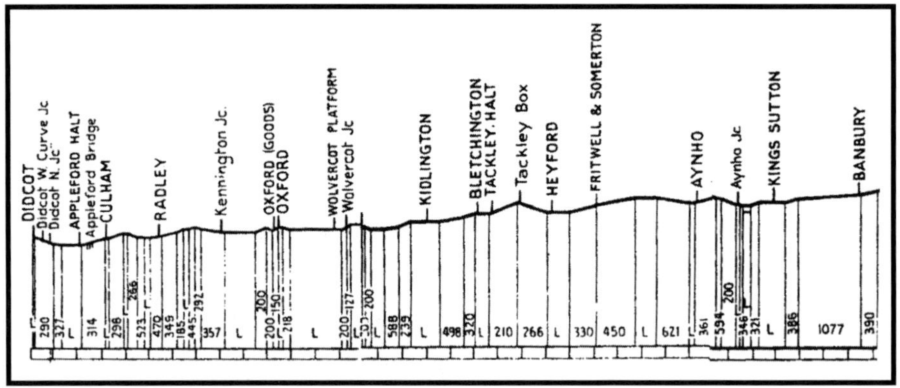

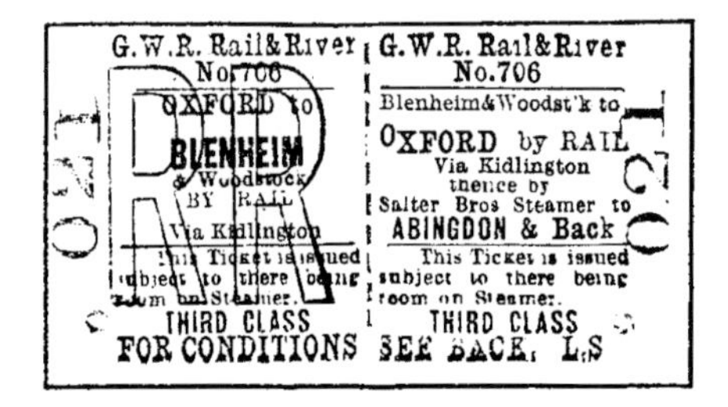

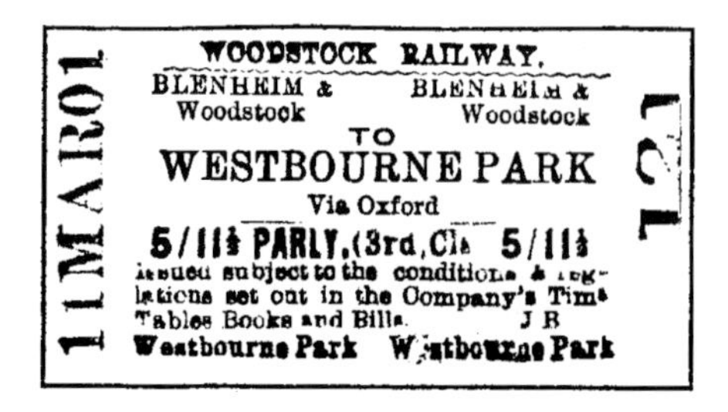

HISTORICAL BACKGROUND

The Great Western Railway reached Reading from London in March 1840 and the line was extended to Steventon (west of Didcot) in June 1840. This became the station for Oxford until a branch from Didcot to the city was opened on 12th June 1844. It was authorised under an Act of Parliament of 11th April 1843 and designed for broad gauge (7ft 0¼ins) by the Oxford Railway Company. The company was purchased by the GWR before work commenced.

Didcot station opened with the branch, which terminated in Oxford near Folly Bridge, on 14th June 1844.

The Oxford & Rugby Railway Company was formed in 1844 and this was acquired by the GWR by the time the single line from Oxford to Banbury was opened on 2nd September 1850. It was doubled in 1852, when a third rail was added for standard gauge trains. Goods traffic did not start until 1853. Trains had to reverse in and out of the terminus at Oxford until the present station came into use on 1st October 1852, which was also the day that the route was extended to Birmingham. It never reached Rugby, however.

The mixed gauge Oxford, Worcester & Wolverhampton Railway opened in 1853 and the London & North Western Railway began running to Oxford from Bletchley in 1851. The OWWR became the West Midland Railway and then, in 1863, part of the GWR. The Didcot-Oxford section became mixed gauge in 1856, but standard gauge running to London was not possible until 1861. Broad gauge traffic in the Oxford area ceased in 1872.

The direct route between Banbury and London was completed in 1910, the junction being at Aynho. The alternative route between Oxford and London via Thame was opened west of that town on 24th October 1864, it joining the original line at Kennington Junction. However, passenger service was withdrawn on 6th January 1963 and through goods traffic ceased in 1965.

Branches

	Opening date	**Closed to passengers**	**Total closure**
Abingdon	2.6.1856	9.9.1963	30.6.1984
Blenheim & Woodstock	19.5.1890	1.3.1954	1.3.1954

The Bletchley line lost its passenger service in 1968, but it was restored as far as Bicester Town in 1987.

There were no major changes when the GWR was nationalised in 1948, to become the Western Region of British Railways. Trains began to appear in sector liveries - InterCity and Network SouthEast - in the mid-1980s - these being followed in the mid-1990s by Thames Trains and Great Western Trains colours as a prelude to privatisation. The former franchise was let on 13th October 1996 and the latter on 4th February of the same year; the owning companies became Victory Railway Holdings and First Group respectively. Virgin CrossCountry trains also run over the route.

The final timetable.

KIDLINGTON and BLENHEIM AND WOODSTOCK—(Third class only)

Week Days only

Miles		a.m T	a.m	a.m		p.m	p.m T	p.m	p.m A	p.m S	p.m B	p.m Y
–	Kidlington............. dep	7 23	8 40	1115	..	1238	3 0	4 10	5 38	5 48	5 53	6 48
2	Shipton-on-Cherwell Halt ..	7 29	8 48	1121	..	1244	3 6	4 16	5 44	5 54	5 59	6 54
3½	Blenheim & Woodstock arr	7 33	8 53	1125	..	1248	3 10	4 20	5 48	5 58	6 3	6 58

Week Days only

Miles		a.m	a.m		p.m	p.m T	p.m	p.m	p.m	p.m		
–	Blenheim & Woodstock dep	7 58	9 30	..	1222	1258	3 48	5 22	6 20	7 10	..	..
1¼	Shipton-on-Cherwell Halt ..	8 4	9 35	..	1227	1 3	3 53	5 27	6 25	7 15	..	..
3½	Kidlington............. arr	8 11	9 40	..	1232	1 8	3 58	5 32	6 30	7 20	..	..

A Except Mondays and Saturdays. B Mondays only. S Saturdays only. T Through service between Oxford and Blenheim & Woodstock (Table 152) Y Runs 6 minutes later on Saturdays commencing 23rd May

PASSENGER SERVICES

Didcot to Banbury

Upon opening, the Didcot to Oxford branch had ten trains on weekdays and five on Sundays, with the 7.30pm departure from Paddington being the only through train from London.

The 1850 extension to Banbury initially had four trains on weekdays. This was increased to six with the extension of the line to Birmingham in 1852.

By 1869, the local train service was largely operated in two sections from Oxford. The table below gives the breakdown in sample years, the proportion of Didcot-Oxford trains originating at Paddington increasing greatly during the 19th century.

	Didcot - Oxford		Oxford - Banbury	
	Weekdays	Sundays	Weekdays	Sundays
1869	10	3	5	3
1880	11	3	5	3
1901	11	5	5	4
1920	12	6	7	3
1940	16	8	9	5
1960	25	10	19	5
1980	32	30	23	18
2000	58	31	26	16

There were also some short workings on the route, notably by steam railmotors north as far as Heyford in the period 1908 to 1916.

Abingdon branch

	Weekdays	Sundays
1870	8	3
1880	10	3
1901	12	3
1920	12	0
1940	16	3
1960	12	4
1963	16	4

Blenheim & Woodstock branch

	Weekdays	Sundays
1890	5	0
1901	5	0
1920	7	0
1940	9	0
1954	10	0

Both branches had some through running to and from Oxford, the number being small each day and varied over the years.

The final timetable.

RADLEY and ABINGDON—(Second class only)

Miles		Week Days																		Sundays			
		am	am S	am	am S	am	am		pm	pm S	pm S	pm S	pm	pm	pm	pm		pm		pm	pm	pm	pm
—	Radley ... dep	7 25	7 50	8 18	9 25	1020	1120	..	1 2	2 50	3 20	4 20	5 8	5 30	6 5	6 40	..	7 28	..	6 35	7 28	9 25	1020
2¼	Abingdon ... arr	7 30	7 55	8 23	9 30	1025	1125	....	1 7	2 55	3 25	4 25	5 13	5 35	6 10	6 45	....	7 33	....	6 40	7 33	9 30	1025

Miles		Week Days																		Sundays			
		am	am S	am	am	am S	am		pm	pm S	pm S	pm S	pm	pm	pm E	pm S	pm	pm		pm	pm		pm
—	Abingdon ... dep	7 5	7 36	8 2	8 27	9 55	11 2	..	1245	1 25	3 0	3 30	4 55	5 17	5 44	5 48	6 25	7 10	..	7 15	9 10	..	10 5
2¼	Radley ... arr	7 10	7 41	8 7	8 32	10 0	11 7	....	1250	1 30	3 5	3 35	5 0	5 22	5 49	5 53	6 30	7 15	....	7 20	9 15	....	1010

S Saturdays only

DIDCOT PARKWAY

III. The 1913 map at 6ins to 1 mile shows only two small villages nearby. The main purpose of the station initially was to serve as a junction for the Oxford branch. The "Loop Line" was used from 22nd December 1856 by expresses between Paddington and The Midlands.

1. The station opened on 12th June 1844 and had a wood-framed roof over its four tracks and six platforms for about 40 years. This postcard view has the entrance to the left of the building on the right. (Lens of Sutton)

2. The station was extensively rebuilt in 1892 to the form seen in this indifferent eastward view. This area was known to railwaymen as "Chester Line Junction", as trains turned north here for that city. (Lens of Sutton)

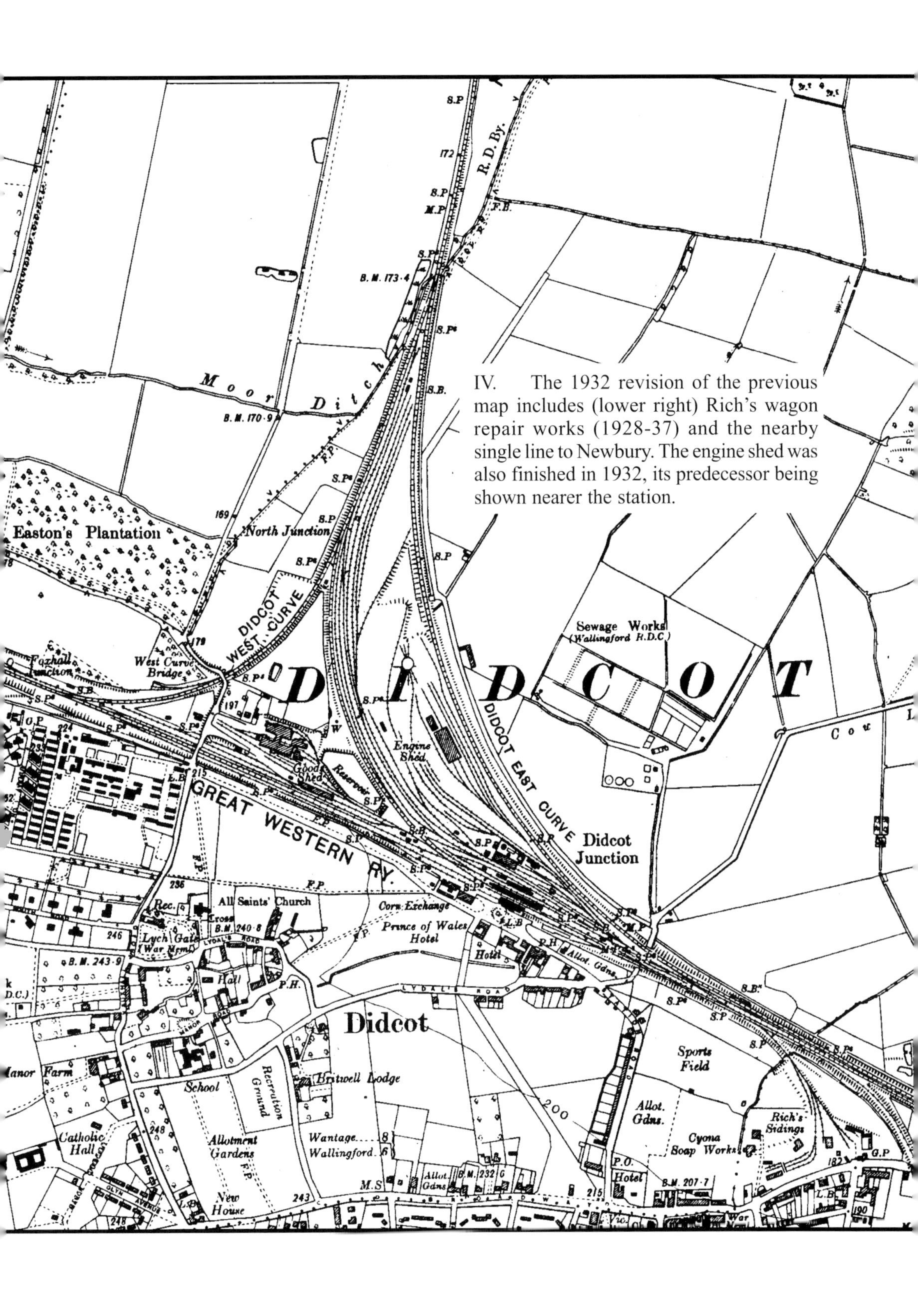

IV. The 1932 revision of the previous map includes (lower right) Rich's wagon repair works (1928-37) and the nearby single line to Newbury. The engine shed was also finished in 1932, its predecessor being shown nearer the station.

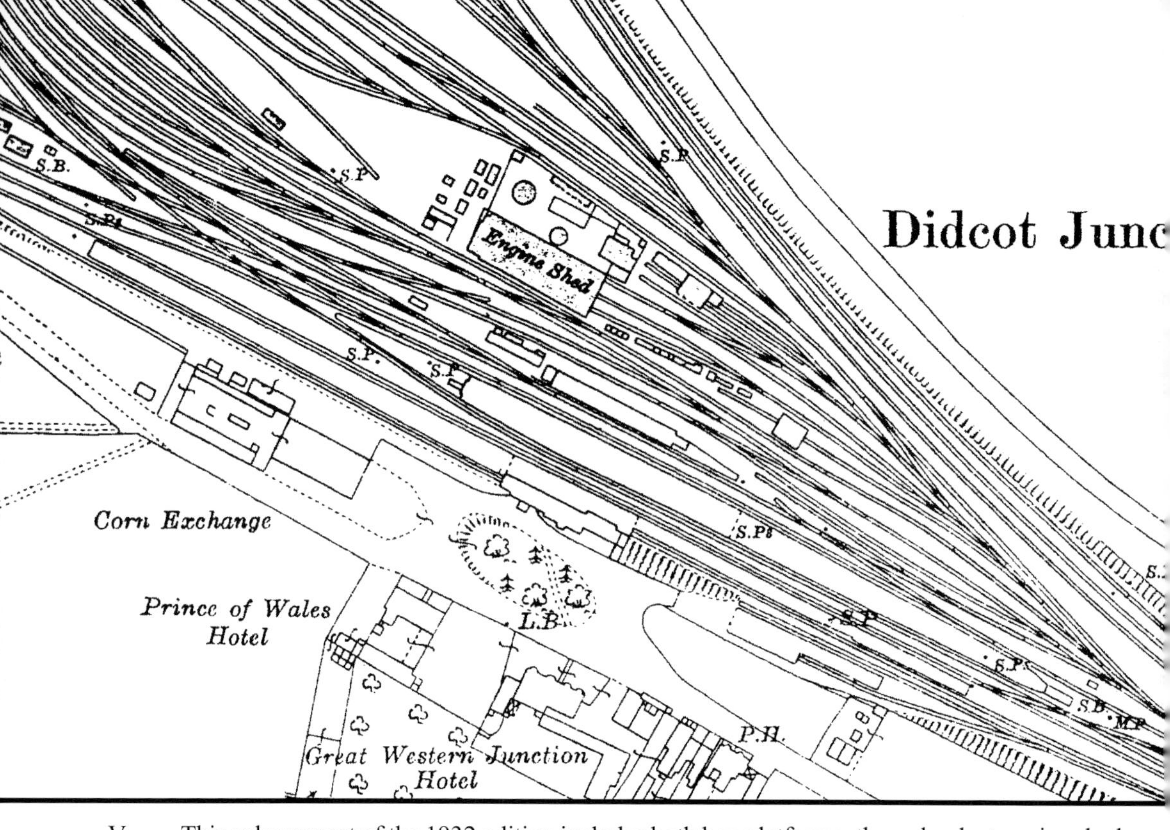

V. This enlargement of the 1932 edition includes both bay platforms, the redundant engine shed and two signal boxes. These were named West End and East End and were closed towards the end of 1932.

3. No. 6910 *Gossington Hall* is entering platform 7 with a train from Oxford on 17th June 1951 and is seen from platform 5. These were renumbered 5 and 3 in 1965, following the closure of the two bays on the south side of the station. (J.H.Moss/R.S.Carpenter coll.)

4. Standing at platform 7 on 12th March 1955 is ex-LSWR class T9 4-4-0 no. 30117 with the 2.56pm Oxford to Southampton train. Its route via Newbury closed in 1964, most trains on it having started from platform 1, the east bay. (S.C.Nash)

5. A stopping train bound for Oxford leaves the 1932 island platform on 2nd April 1988, with no. 37131 standing on the left. The main lines through the station were quadrupled in 1932. This location had been renamed "Oxford Line Junction". (T.Heavyside)

6. No. 50026 *Indomitable* was recorded on 22nd June 1990, while working the 17.00 Oxford to Paddington service in Network SouthEast livery. Also evident is much of West Yard and part of the Didcot Power Station complex, which accounts for so many coal hoppers being present. (M.J.Stretton)

7. The down side buildings (right) were rebuilt in 1985 and the suffix "Parkway" was applied on 29th July when the new accommodation was opened. The steam on the left is from the cylinder drain cocks of a locomotive near the end of the demonstration line of the Didcot Railway Centre, which is fully described in our *Reading to Didcot* album. No. 6024 *King Edward I* departs with the 'Cotswold Venturer' on 22nd August 1993. (T.Heavyside)

8. To complete our brief survey of Didcot, we have three 2002 views, necessarily taken against the light. EWS opened a diesel refuelling and servicing depot in April 1994 on the vacant site seen on the left of picture 6. (V.Mitchell)

Other Middleton Press albums to feature this station:
Didcot to Swindon
Didcot to Winchester
Reading to Didcot

9. The diesel depot is in the background of this panorama which includes a coal train for Didcot Power Station on West Curve and engineers wagons in West Sidings. The Didcot Railway Centre were planning to acquire some of these sidings. (V.Mitchell)

10. Travelling a little further north we come to the junction with Didcot East Curve, on which a down freight train is waiting. Below the lone railway observer can be seen the Transfer Shed, an important exhibit at the Didcot Railway Centre. Until 1977, it had stood west of the station and had served as the goods shed. It had been built as The Tranship Shed for broad and standard gauge goods exchange. (V.Mitchell)

SOUTH OF APPLEFORD

11. About ½ mile south of Appleford Halt was Appleford Crossing signal box, it controlling gates over a minor road. The box had to be rebuilt after an accident in 1952 and ceased to be a block post in 1965. (Lens of Sutton coll.)

12. Lifting barriers were installed in 1982 and the 22-lever frame box was demolished in 2002. No. L205 was working the 11.15 Banbury to Reading service on 18th May 1992 and was nearing the end of its career. (M.J.Stretton)

13. A facing point in the down main line north of the crossing came into use in October 1976 to serve the Amey sidings and refuse terminal. From November 1973 until that time, there had been a trailing connection further north. The crossover in the foreground of this 2002 photo also dates from late 1976. The box had been demolished recently. (V.Mitchell)

14. A westward panorama from the gantry crane on 29th November 2002 shows one of the crane's rails and part of the 22.59 train from Brentford. It comprised about 30 twin FLA units each carrying six waste containers, which are unloaded for emptying in the landfill site of the Waste Recycling Group. (M.J.Stretton)

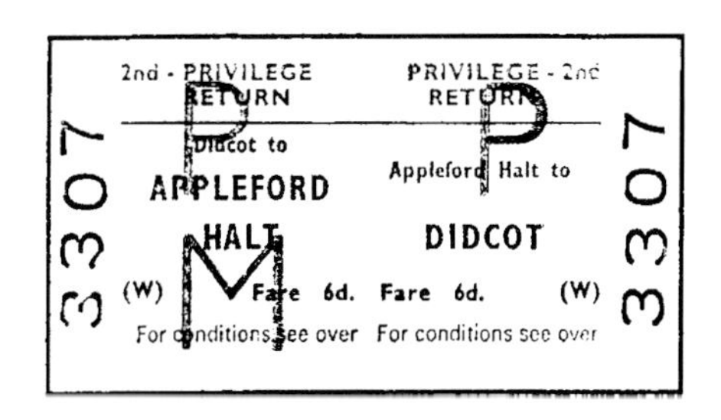

APPLEFORD

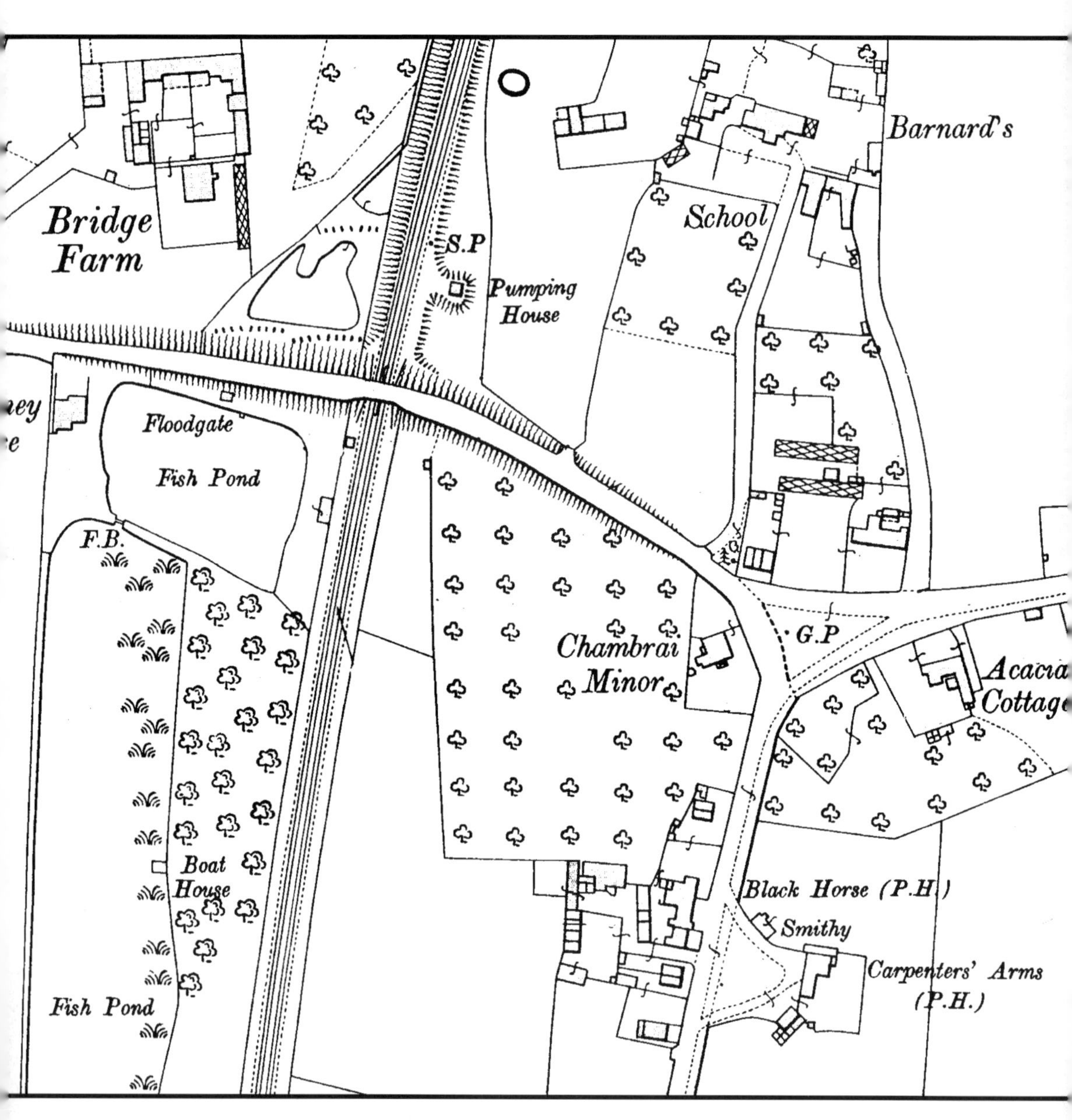

VI. The 1912 map shows the bridge south of which a halt was opened on 11th September 1933. The 1901 census had shown a population of only 251 here.

15. A northward view on 8th June 1957 reveals the standard GWR timber platforms adorned with their distinctive Pagoda shelters. There had been a station called Appleford Crossing from 1844 to 1849. (H.C.Casserley)

16. Seen on the same day is the helpful sign, also a poster for an early "Steam Traction Engine Rally", which was held in the village. The post is a former broad gauge rail. The suffix "Halt" was dropped from 5th May 1969. (H.C.Casserley)

17. No. 43070 was at the front of the 08.18 Manchester Piccadilly to Bournemouth HST on 18th May 1992. Shown in the timetable as "The Pines Express", it sadly no longer carried the traditional headboard. However, little had changed at this location, apart from the lighting. (M.J.Stretton)

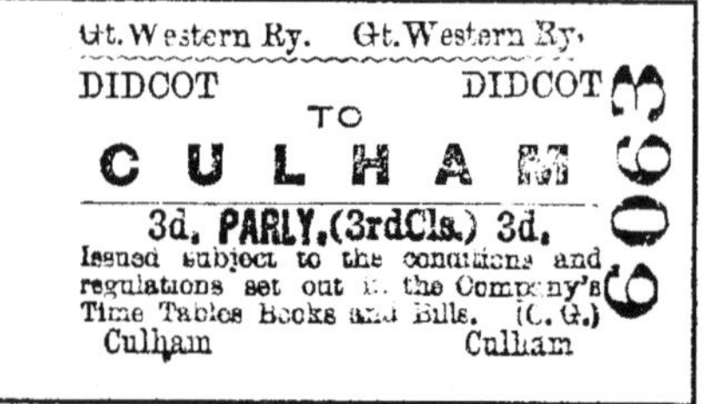

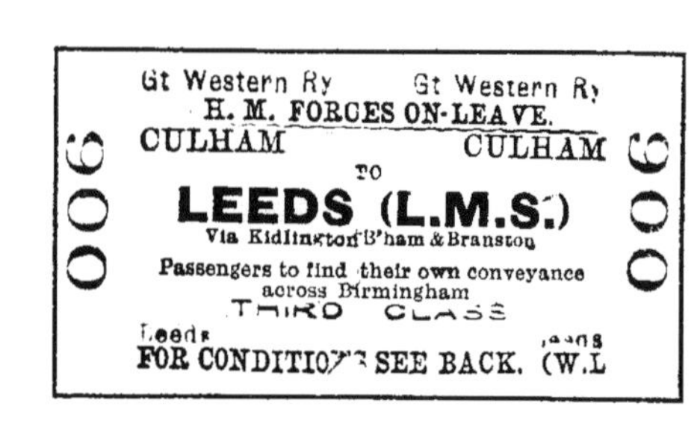

CULHAM

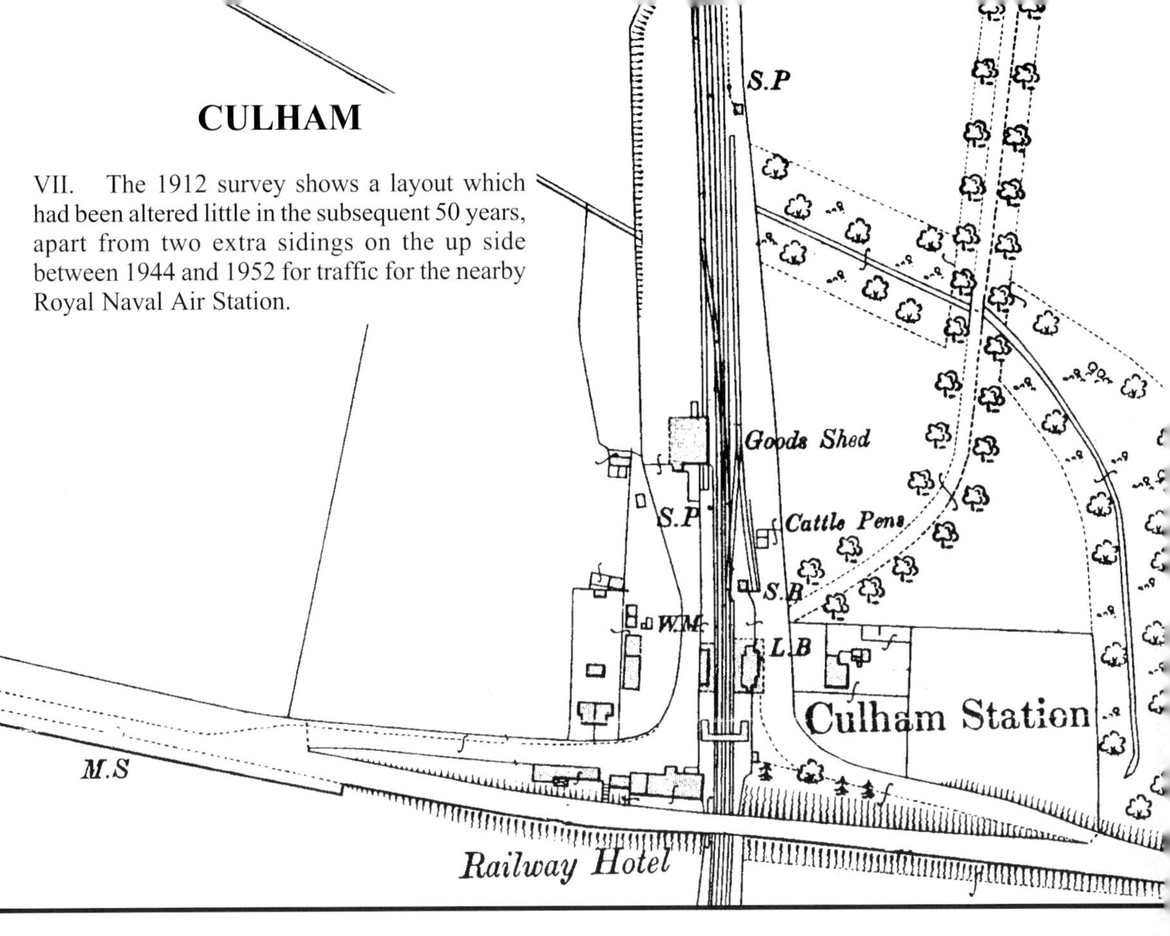

VII. The 1912 survey shows a layout which had been altered little in the subsequent 50 years, apart from two extra sidings on the up side between 1944 and 1952 for traffic for the nearby Royal Naval Air Station.

18. A 1919 northward view includes the up refuge siding and an ivy covered signal box. The station was named "Abingdon Road" until 1856, when the branch to that town opened. There was a staff of 9 or 10 here between the wars. (LGRP/NRM)

19. The goods yard was closed on 19th July 1965, although it had handled only coal in the previous nine months. The signal box was rebuilt in 1952 and is seen in 1959. It was closed on 12th February 1961 and had a 29-lever frame. (R.M.Casserley)

20. The 07.18 Manchester Piccadilly to Poole speeds through on 2nd June 1990 behind a class 47 diesel. The loss of the footbridge roof was the main visual change here. (P.G.Barnes)

Culham	1903	1913	1923	1933
Passenger tickets issued	15693	17453	14406	10029
Season tickets issued	*	*	67	94
Parcels forwarded	10670	15653	10901	14391
General goods forwarded (tons)	3170	3004	3197	558
Coal and coke received (tons)	300	461	475	302
Other minerals received (tons)	1434	847	1250	923
General goods received (tons)	1541	2036	1383	932
Trucks of livestock handled	74	94	80	64

(* not available.)

21. The chalet-style main building from the Brunel era was recorded on the same day, by which time it was a listed structure. The timetable posters are headed "Thames Line". (P.G.Barnes)

22. The introduction of Thames Turbos with one-person-operation in the early 1990s necessitated the provision of mirrors and a new platform. There were visual restrictions on the old platform - this is the untidy result from blinkered planners. (M.J.Stretton)

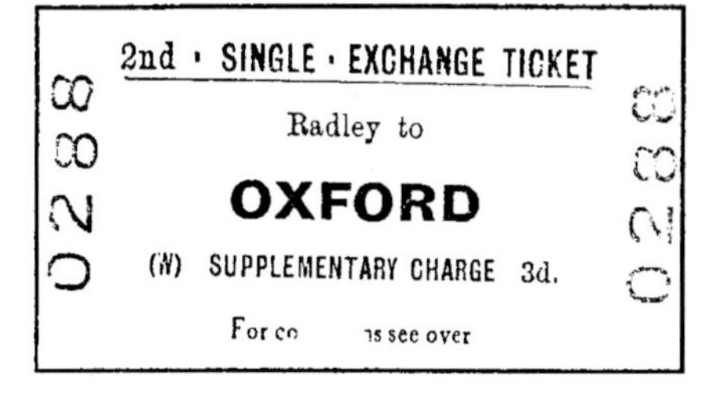

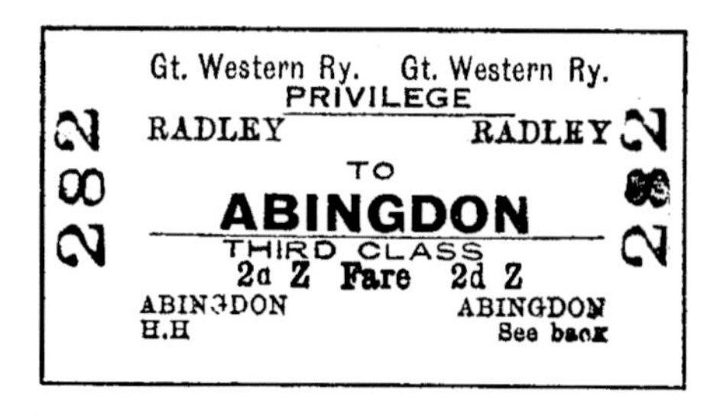

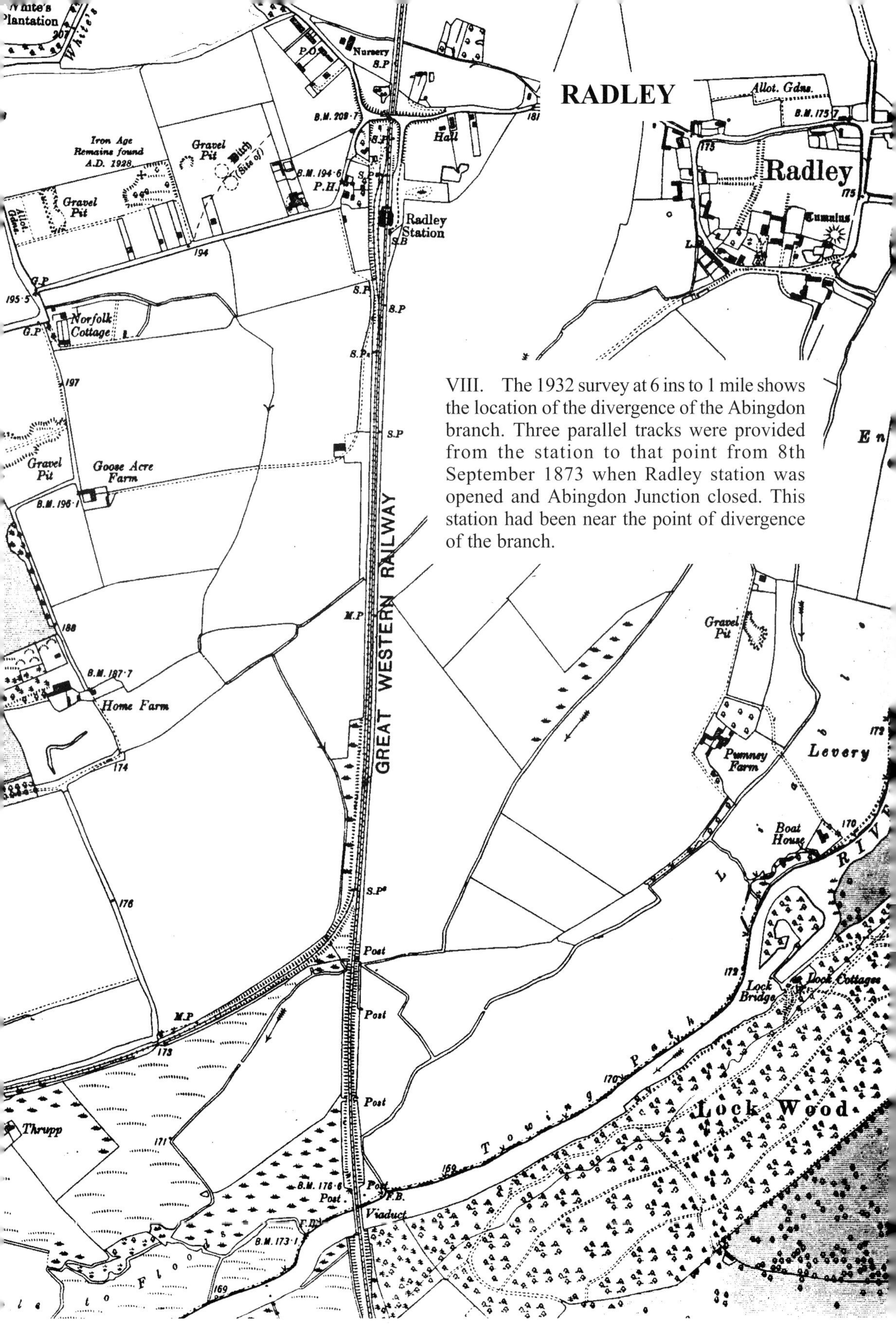

VIII. The 1932 survey at 6 ins to 1 mile shows the location of the divergence of the Abingdon branch. Three parallel tracks were provided from the station to that point from 8th September 1873 when Radley station was opened and Abingdon Junction closed. This station had been near the point of divergence of the branch.

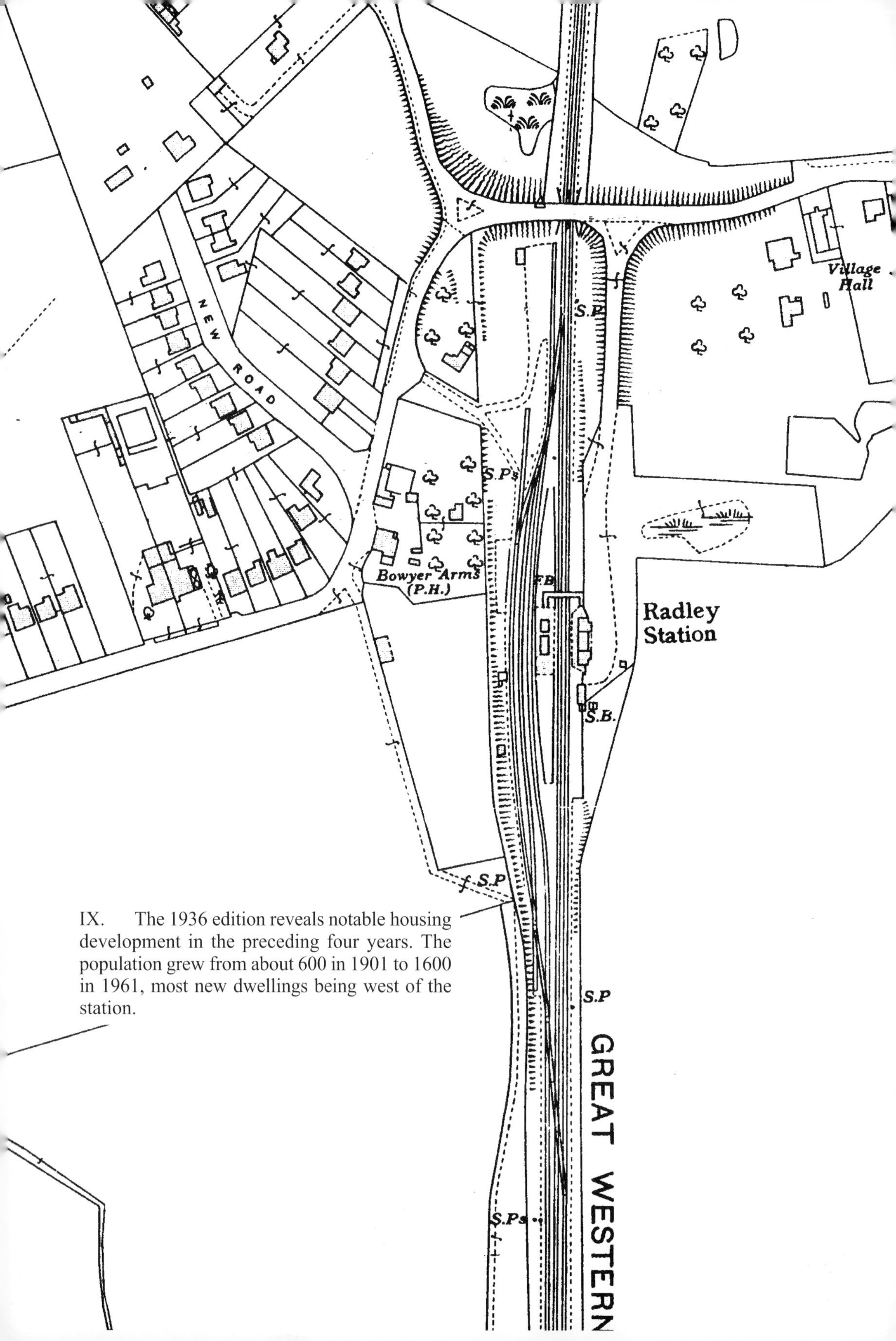

IX. The 1936 edition reveals notable housing development in the preceding four years. The population grew from about 600 in 1901 to 1600 in 1961, most new dwellings being west of the station.

23. Our earliest view of an Abingdon branch train shows four-wheeled coaches standing on bridge rail, in all probability of broad gauge origin. The locomotive is no. 1306 and came from the Monmouthshire Railway & Canal Company in 1880. It was built in 1872 and was used on the branch in 1901. (Lens of Sutton coll.)

24. A southward panorama from the road bridge includes the roadway to the main buildings on the up side. There were six or seven men employed here for most of the first half of the 20th century. (Lens of Sutton coll.)

25. Still showing its SR no. of 746, class N15 4-6-0 *Pendragon* blows off as it runs through on 18th June 1949 with a Sheffield to Bournemouth express. The signal box closed on 21st May 1965; it had a 41-lever frame. (J.H.Meredith)

→

26. The branch train was composed of no. 5816 with autocoach no. W185W on 28th May 1957. Curiously, the locomotive was not fitted for autotrain working. The goods yard remained open until 27th June 1971, although only used for coal after 1964. (R.M.Casserley)

Radley	1903	1913	1923	1933
Passenger tickets issued	17846	14507	15594	7614
Season tickets issued	*	11	34	34
Parcels forwarded	5306	7763	3806	4643
General goods forwarded (tons)	376	326	331	129
Coal and coke received (tons)	4	107	65	438
Other minerals received (tons)	565	270	620	562
General goods received (tons)	439	298	363	317
Trucks of livestock handled	-	-	4	15

(* not available.)

→

27. The footbridge was an ideal place from which to observe southbound expresses, such as this one hauled by no. 7026 *Tenby Castle* in 1958. It will soon pass the site of Nuneham signal box, which was in use from 1940 until 1953 and had only six levers. (J.W.T.House/C.L.Caddy)

RADLEY

28. In pristine condition, no. 9773 approaches the station with MG cars from the factory at Abingdon on 17th August 1965. There were no signal arms on the posts, as the box had recently closed. A ground frame was subsequently provided north of the island platform. (G.P.Cooper)

29. Regular passenger services to Abingdon had ceased in 1963, but a DMU shuttle was operated from 23rd to 25th May 1970, as part of the Abingdon Festival. The connection to the down line was moved from the far end of the platform to behind the camera on 25th February 1973. (S.P.Derek)

30. No. 50035 *Ark Royal* heads the 15.00 Paddington to Hereford service on 25th September 1981, having run alongside the Abingdon branch evident in the distance. This continued in use until June 1984. Passengers now have direct access to the down platform. In a little over one mile, the train would reach the site of Sandford signal box which had 34 levers and was in use from 7th April 1940 until 14th December 1964. There was quadruple track northwards during that period. (T.Heavyside)

RADLEY

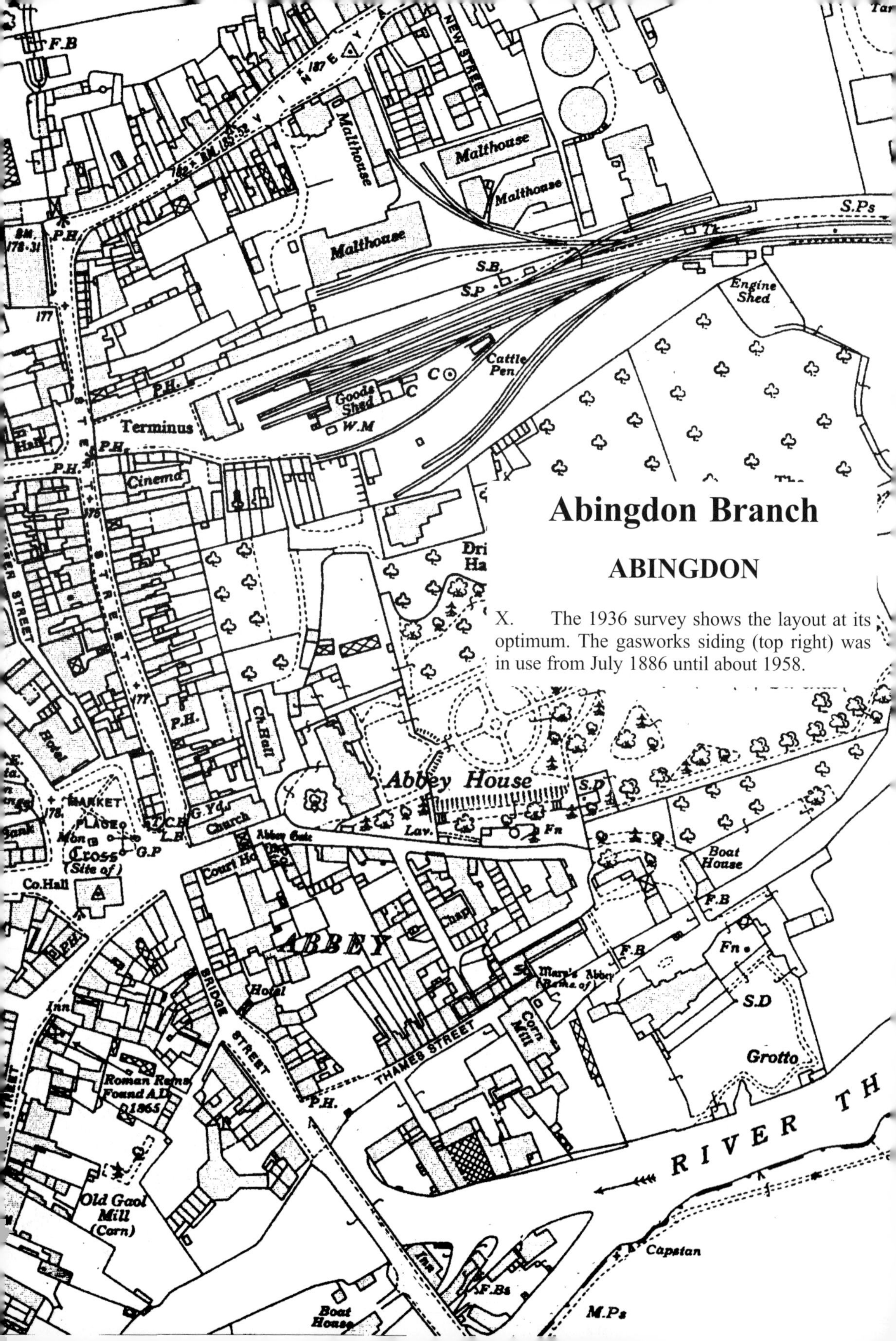

Abingdon Branch

ABINGDON

X. The 1936 survey shows the layout at its optimum. The gasworks siding (top right) was in use from July 1886 until about 1958.

Abingdon	1903	1913	1923	1933
Passenger tickets issued	59496	62660	44289	22244
Season tickets issued	*	193	375	100
Parcels forwarded	48264	57705	48570	54974
General goods forwarded (tons)	7517	6783	6936	2343
Coal and coke received (tons)	1668	942	3044	2972
Other minerals received (tons)	5032	4883	2699	4467
General goods received (tons)	13451	14638	14860	8279
Trucks of livestock handled	152	349	329	346

(* not available.)

31. Broad gauge stock of this type was in use on the branch until its conversion in November 1872. The 0-6-0T is one of the "Leo" class introduced by Gooch in 1842. (British Railways)

32. A photograph from 1919 includes the 2½ milepost and limewashed cattle wagons. At around this time, the usual branch engine was a 0-4-2T of the 517 class. The population of the town rose from 6480 in 1901 to 15,200 in 1961. (LGRP/NRM)

33. This panorama includes the goods crane (listed as of 8-ton capacity in 1938), the maltings and its siding (right) and the signalman in the box which had 18 levers. There was a staff of 20 for most of the 1930s. (LGRP/NRM)

34. The wooden station building was extensively damaged in a shunting accident on 22nd April 1908 and subsequently demolished. Seen in 1949, the replacement structure lasted into the 1970s. (J.H.Meredith)

35. Three photographs from 1958 reveal more details of this little known terminus. By this time, the City of Oxford AECs (right) had gobbled up most of the passengers. MG cars were being loaded into the vans (left), the first having been produced by Cecil Kimber in 1923. The initials referred to Morris Garages, the wood and fabric bodies being allied to many Morris parts. The widely popular "Midget" came out in 1929. (B.W.Leslie/Great Western Society)

36. This eastward view includes the cattle dock and part of the gasworks siding, visible between the signal box and the water tank. The engine shed had been to the right of the latter, but was closed on 20th March 1954. (B.W.Leslie/Great Western Society)

37. After 1947, the 1400 and 5800 class 0-4-2Ts provided power on the branch until dieselisation in the 1960s. No. 1420 is departing with an unusual item of passenger's luggage which was too big for the van. The nearby Thames attracted many visitors. The locomotive now serves tourists on the South Devon Railway. (A.E.Bennett)

38. The MG car factory closed in 1980, but coal for Charrington's depot continued to arrive by rail until 1984. This kept the branch open. A single railcar was photographed on 28th April 1962, its class being 121. (F.Hornby)

39. As part of the Abingdon Festival on 23rd May 1970, the Great Western Society moved many items of stock from Didcot to create an exhibition lasting three days. Included in the show were 0-4-2T no. 1466, 2-6-2T no. 6106 (both illustrated), *Pendennis Castle*, *Earl Bathurst*, *Burton Agnes Hall* and *Shannon*. The DMU shuttled to Radley every half hour. Three trips from Oxford by a DMU marked the end of the branch on 30th June 1984. (S.P.Derek)

SOUTH OF OXFORD

XI. The 1900 edition has the GWR through station and the LNWR terminus top left. The alignment of the branch to the first GWR station is indicated by two boundary fences at the bottom of the map. The line continued along Marlborough Road to the river bank, although the passenger station was at the end of Western Road. The line for the Oxford Gas, Light and Coke Company is near the centre of the map and came into use on 13th May 1886. An additional siding complex, further south, was opened in 1924. All the lines ceased to carry coal in 1960, but were used occasionally until 1967. Hinksey North signal box was nearby and was in use from 1942 until 1973. The map shows the previous box, Oxford South; to the north of it is South End Yard.

40. No. 35023 *Holland-Afrika Line* was bound for Bournemouth when recorded passing Kennington Junction signal box on 17th August 1965. The line from Princes Risborough is under the second coach. The down goods line (left) had been taken out of use three months earlier. Part of the branch remains in use to the Cowley car factory. The box had 43 levers and was open from 1901 to 1973. (G.P.Cooper)

41. Abingdon Road Halt was next on our journey into Oxford, but it was in use from only 1st February 1908 to 22nd March 1915. The track was quadrupled in this vicinity in 1942 for wartime traffic. (Lens of Sutton coll.)

42. A view north from Abingdon Road bridge on 17th August 1963 features no. 7824 *Iford Manor* with the 10.30am Birmingham Snow Hill to Hastings train. It ran via Guildford (Saturdays only) and arrived at 4.41pm. Behind it is Hinksey South signal box, which was in use from 29th March 1942 to 18th December 1973. It had an amazing 72 levers, whilst Hinksey North had 69. This was in use over the same period. (E.Wilmshurst)

43. A southward view from the same bridge on 31st March 1988 includes no. 58009 with empty coal hoppers from Didcot Power Station. There were about 17 such coal trains per day from the Midlands, six days a week for much of the 1980s. The four tracks reduce to three under the A423. (T.Heavyside)

44. The Abingdon Road bridge is in the background of this southward panorama from July 2001. The 20 sidings of Hinksey Yard had been laid down in 1942, but most were not used after 1967. Only six remained in 1974. The yard became the Railtrack Virtual Quarry and was relaid in 2001. Hinksey Halt had been nearby from 1908 to 1915. The junction for Oxford's original station had been in this vicinity. (M.J.Stretton)

45. No. 47252 approaches the station on 4th October 1975 with a Paddington to Worcester train. This location is known to many frustrated passengers as "Graveyard Halt", as many trains are stopped by signals near the cemetery on the right. On the left is the goods shed that was once an important part of South End Yard. It was demolished in 1985. (T.Heavyside)

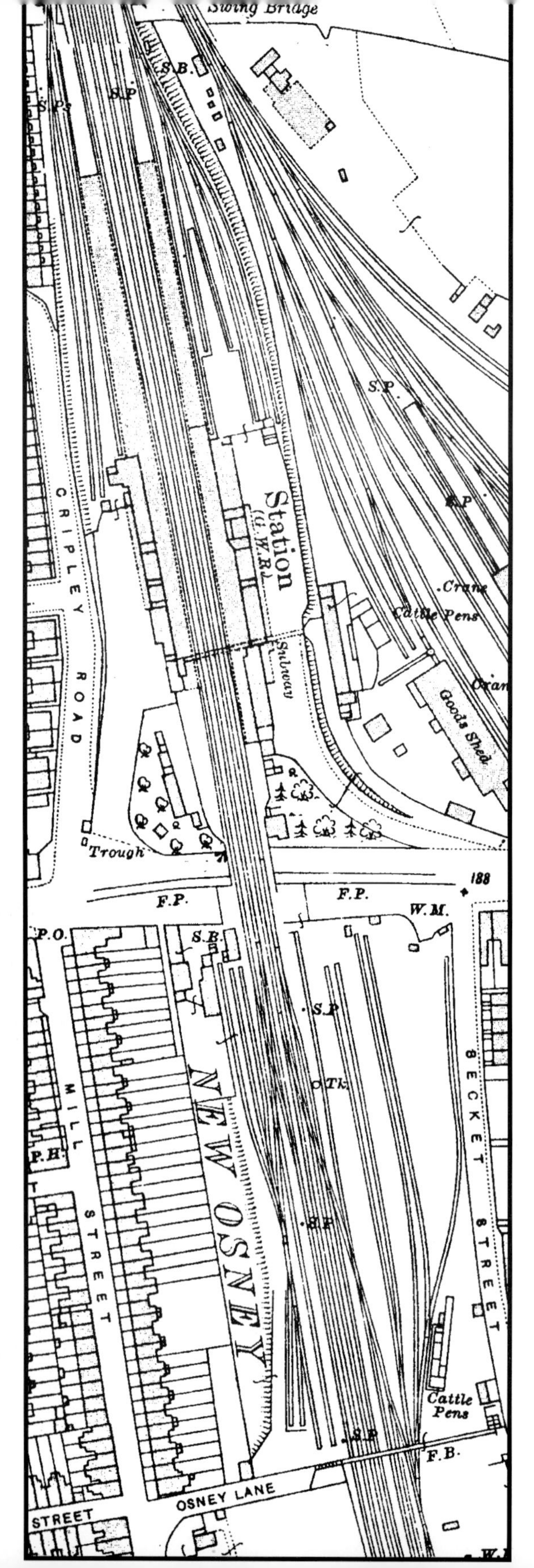

OXFORD

XIIa. The 1921 survey includes Becket Street Goods Yard (lower right), which became the site of an ugly scrapyard in the 1980s. It is now the station car park. South End Yard began at the lower border of this map. On the right of the upper part are the LNWR lines of Rewley Road station, which was used by passengers from the Bletchley line until 1951.

46. The first station on the present site opened in 1852, the terminus closing on 1st October of that year. It had a roof over the tracks and a bay at the north end for OWWR trains. The roof was removed in November 1890 and the station was rebuilt to the form seen during the following 12 months. The main buildings were erected on the up side and are seen in 1911. Like the originals, they were of timber construction, and they lasted into the 1970s, although in poor condition by that time. (Lens of Sutton)

47. A northward view from the signal box includes the bridge over Botley Road, which had a headroom of only 13ft 6ins. The bridge was raised in 1979, but the bypass level crossing for tall vehicles was retained. Mid-platform scissors crossings were in use for some years, these allowing two short trains at each platform simultaneously. (LGRP/NRM)

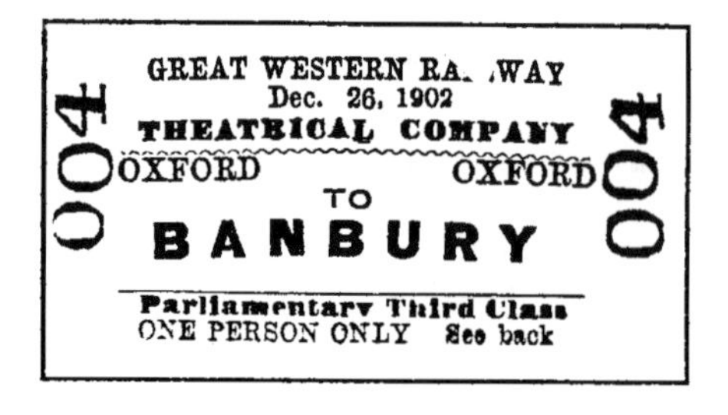
GREAT WESTERN RA. .WAY
Dec. 26, 1902
THEATRICAL COMPANY
004 OXFORD TO OXFORD 004
BANBURY
Parliamentary Third Class
ONE PERSON ONLY See back

STATION
Summer
Tickets

48. A southward view in 1919 includes one of the scissors crossovers, but only one half of it appears to have been used regularly. The bay on the right was used by Fairford and Woodstock branch trains. There was a staff of 315 employed on passenger and goods activities at Oxford in 1929, this figure excluding the locomotive and engineering departments. (LGRP/NRM)

49. A Woodstock train stands alongside the two carriage sidings, which were in place until 1968. Seen on 9th April 1927 with trailer no. 99 is no. 1473 *Fair Rosamund*. It was unusual for a GWR tank engine to carry a name. (H.C.Casserley)

50. No. 2270 passes over Botley Road on 8th June 1957 with a northbound freight, its tender being on the emergency level crossing. On the left is part of Becket Street Yard and on the right is the 1908 Station South signal box, which was named "Oxford Goods" until 1942. It had 57 levers and was in use until 29th October 1973. (H.C.Casserley)

OXFOR

51. Another northbound goods was recorded later the same month, but this is passing Station North box. The class G2a 0-8-0 7F had worked for the LMS for most of its life. Its number is 49330 and it is passing over the link between the River Thames and the Oxford Canal. (R.M.Casserley)

52. Running south over the same bridge on 23rd July 1961 is no. 5167 with the 11.5am stopping train from Banbury to Oxford. The timber-built engine shed is on the left. It was closed on 31st December 1965 and demolished in 1968. The OWWR shed of 1854 is to the left of the smokebox. (P.J.Kelley)

53. One of the Intercity diesel units stands at the up platform on 7th July 1971, during the rebuilding period in which this temporary scaffold footbridge was provided. Part of the dull new CLASP structure is visible; it was cheap, plain, unsuited for an elegant city and rotted within 20 years. The station became a fraudster's paradise when barriers were removed in 1985; they have recently been replaced! (H.C.Casserley)

5167
PASSENGERS MUST
NOT CROSS THE LINE
EXCEPT BY MEANS
OF THE SUBWAY

1A

54. The 100-lever Station North box had been called "Engine Shed Signal Box" until 1942 and remained in use until 1973. This photograph was taken from almost the same point as no. 52, but on 4th October 1975. No. 31260 is passing over the rebuilt bridge; the diesel depot is on the left, this closing in 1984. (T.Heavyside)

55. The abolition of signal boxes was achieved by fitting a panel into a small building near the down platform (left); it came into partial use on 7th October 1973. A carriage shed with three roads once stood on the siding area on the left. No. 47848 is leaving with the 16.15 Liverpool Lime Street to Poole on 12th July 1990. A bay platform (no. 3) was retained at the far end of the up platform. (M.J.Stretton)

56. From the same viewpoint as nos. 52 and 54, we witness a Thames Turbo leaving the new berthing sidings east of the main line on 18th May 1992, about to form the 11.00 departure to Paddington. The earlier carriage sidings on the left were retained. Note that the signals allowed for reversible running. The total staff at Oxford in 1985 was 209, which included 51 drivers. (M.J.Stretton)

Other pictures of this station can be seen in *Branch Line to Fairford* (Middleton Press).

OX
82
165106

57. Freight traffic increases necessitated signalling alterations to reduce headways from seven to three minutes; the work was scheduled to last until September 2003. No. 66533 is on the up through line working the 04.32 Garston to Southampton Docks, while a Virgin Voyager stands at the down platform while running from Poole to Newcastle. The station was rebuilt in a modern and distinctive style, opening on 8th April 1990. A pleasant glazed footbridge replaced the often-overcrowded subway. (M.J.Stretton)

A.M.
GREAT WESTERN RAILWAY.
OXFORD (A) STATION
Admit ONE to Platform 1d
This ticket must be given up on leaving the platform
Available One hour.
For conditions see back.
P.M.
1 | 2 | 3 | 4 | 5 | 6 | 7 | 8 | 9 | 10 | 11 | 12
88220

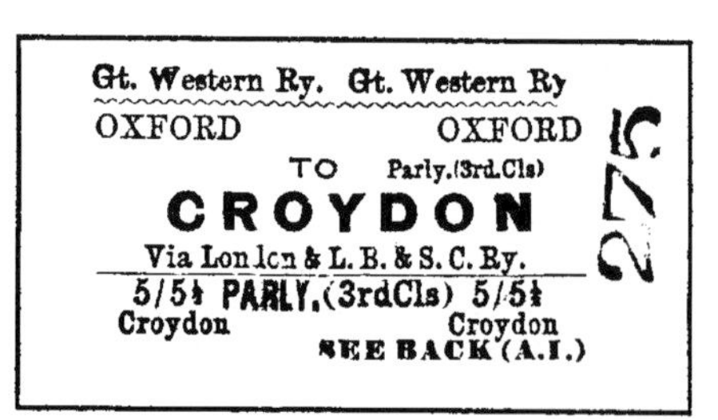
Gt. Western Ry. Gt. Western Ry
OXFORD OXFORD
TO Parly.(3rd.Cls)
CROYDON
Via London & L. B. & S. C. Ry.
5/5½ PARLY.(3rdCls) 5/5½
Croydon Croydon
SEE BACK (A.I.)
2275

OXFORD SHED

58. The WMR built a three-road shed for standard gauge locomotives in 1862 alongside the existing OWWR single road shed. A lifting shop was added in 1875. Station North box and two of the first generation railcars (nos. W15W and W4W) were recorded on 22nd February 1953. (B.W.L.Brooksbank/Initial Photographics)

59. A panorama from the coal stage in June 1965 includes nos 5971, 90687, 48641, the lofty lifting shop and Station North box. There were 280 footplate men here in the 1950s, plus 155 other staff in the depot. (C.Stacey/Initial Photographics)

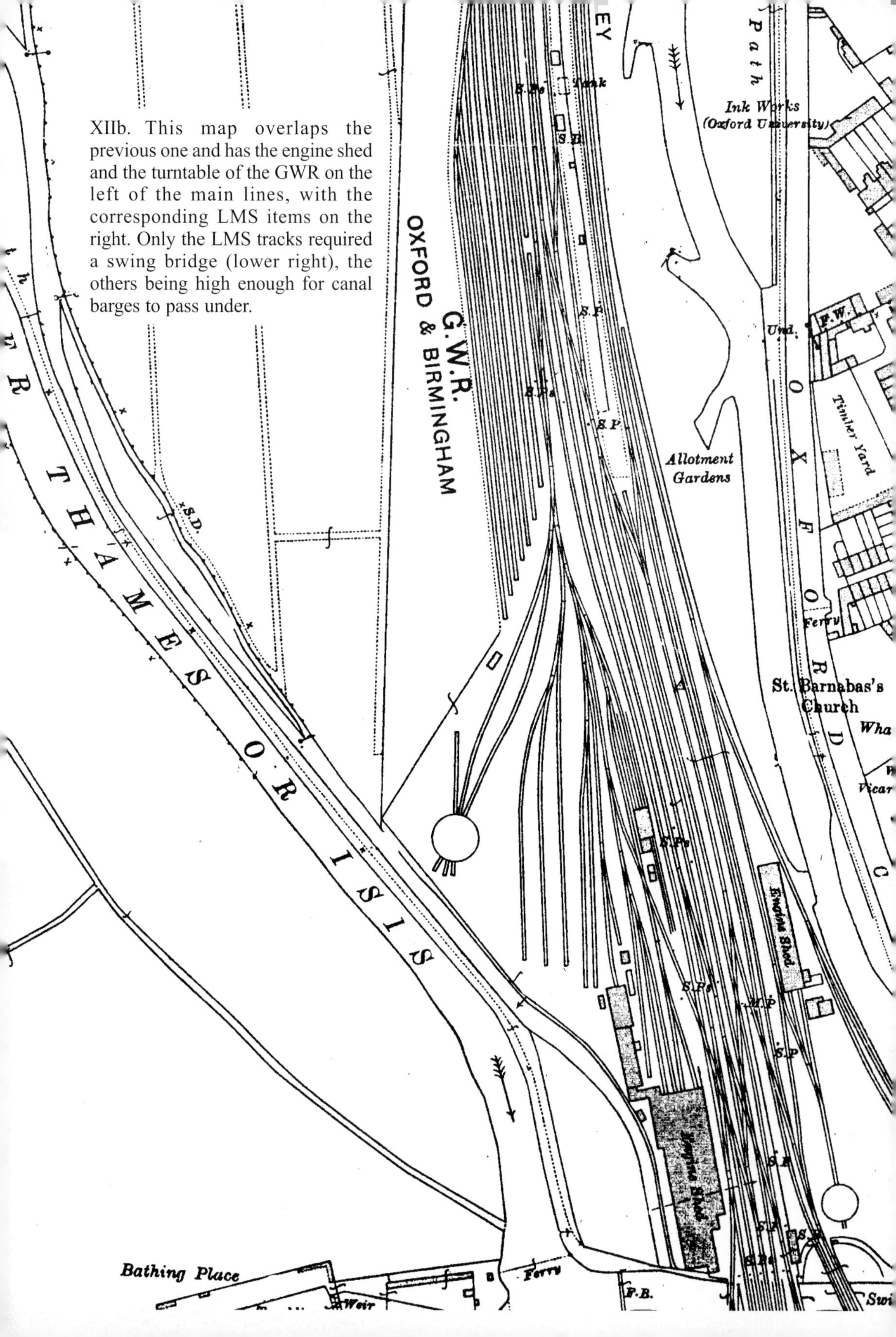

XIIb. This map overlaps the previous one and has the engine shed and the turntable of the GWR on the left of the main lines, with the corresponding LMS items on the right. Only the LMS tracks required a swing bridge (lower right), the others being high enough for canal barges to pass under.

60. This double-sided coaling stage was built in 1944 and many extra sidings were laid to cope with wartime demands, particularly for D-Day. The old single coal stage was north of the shed, whereas this one was north of the turntable. No. 34093 *Saunton* was taking water on 30th October 1965, ready to return to the Southern Region. (S.C.Nash)

61. The diesel depot was a simpler affair, but the old water tank was retained beyond the fuel tanks. The shed was used during refuelling. This was undertaken at Reading after 1984. In the late 1960s, the allocation included Type 3 Hymeks, NBL Type 2s and class 08 shunters. This photograph is from 23rd April 1987. (M.J.Stretton)

NORTH OF OXFORD

62. The middle of this northbound train is at Oxford North Junction, which was created on 3rd November 1940 when the two tracks, partly obscured by smoke, were opened to provide a connection with the LMS Bletchley line (left). The previous link was through exchange sidings nearer Oxford. From 1974, it was further north and all the ex-LNWR route to Rewley Road terminus was removed. This 1954 view features no. 7900 *St. Peter's Hall*. The 88-lever signal box, which is largely obscured by the water tank, was in use from 1940 to 1973. (A.W.V.Mace/Milepost 92½ Picture Library)

63. Moving further north, we reach the point where the down goods loop is separated from the three other ex-GWR tracks. The ex-LMS tracks (in the background) were quadrupled in this area and controlled by Port Meadow signal box (above the penultimate coach) from 1941 to 1960. No. 7404 is hauling a train from Fairford on 11th March 1946. (H.C.Casserley)

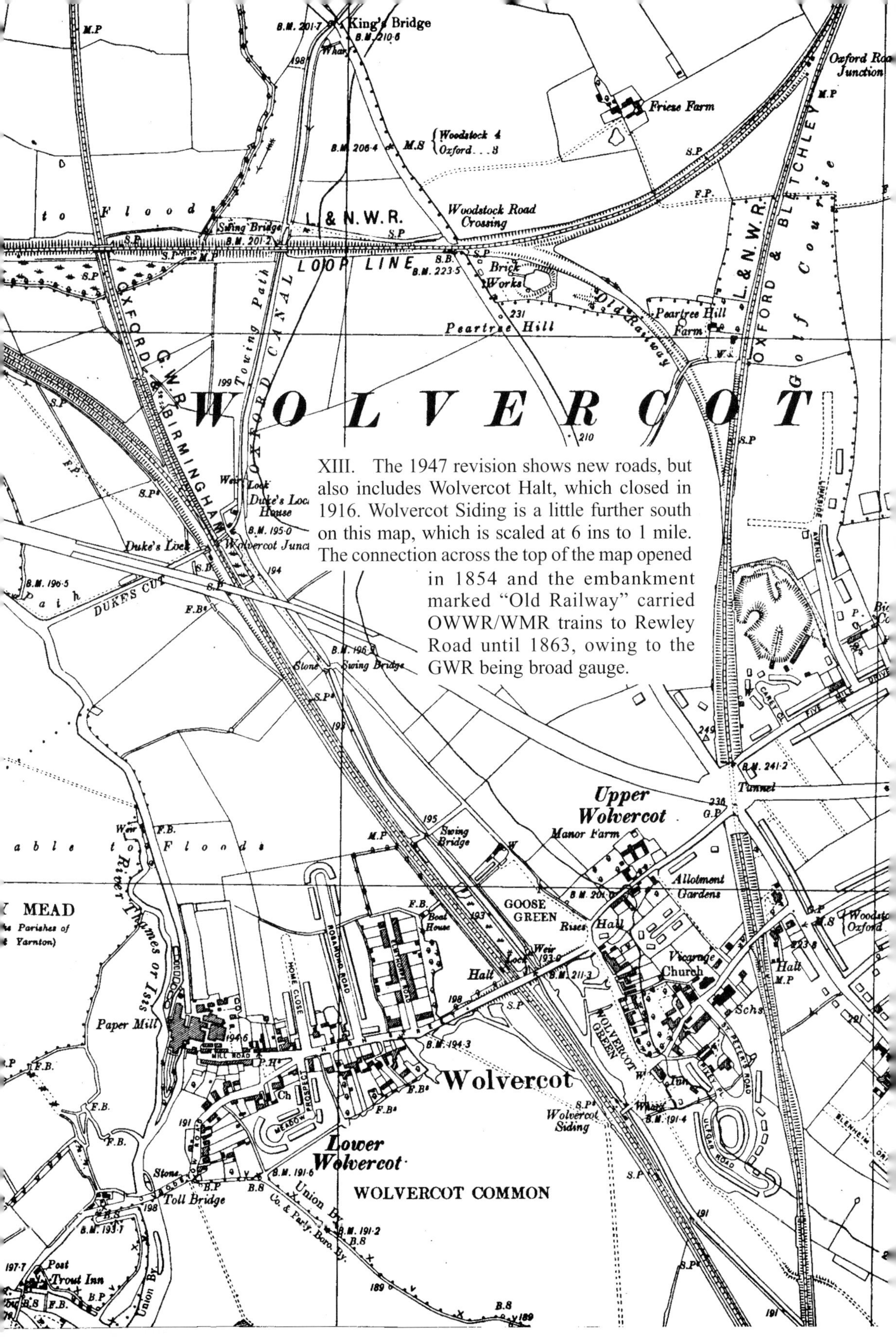

XIII. The 1947 revision shows new roads, but also includes Wolvercot Halt, which closed in 1916. Wolvercot Siding is a little further south on this map, which is scaled at 6 ins to 1 mile. The connection across the top of the map opened in 1854 and the embankment marked "Old Railway" carried OWWR/WMR trains to Rewley Road until 1863, owing to the GWR being broad gauge.

64. A public siding was provided at Wolvercot until 9th June 1958, although it was between the down main and down goods loop after 1942. Wolvercot Siding box was on the east of the tracks and had a 29-lever frame. It closed with the siding. (Lens of Sutton)

65. Wolvercot Halt was open from 1st February 1908 and was served by steam railmotors until closure on 1st January 1916. Wolvercote is the present spelling and the LNWR preferred this on their nearby halt. (Lens of Sutton)

66. The 35-lever Wolvercot Junction box was photographed in the 1950s, with the Worcester line curving to the left and the Loop Line on the embankment. The branch to the left was singled in 1971 and the box was closed in October 1973. (Lens of Sutton coll.)

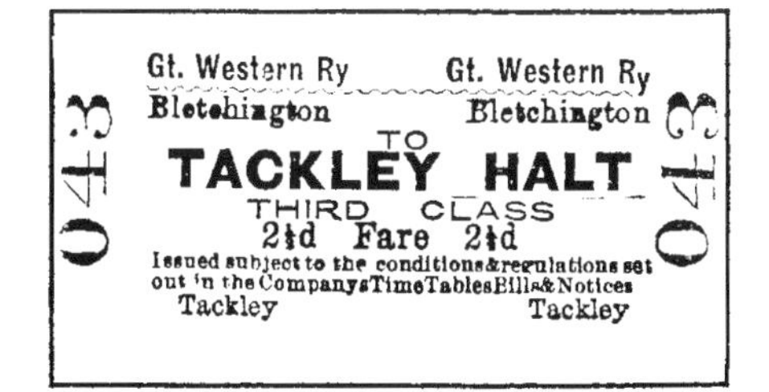

KIDLINGTON

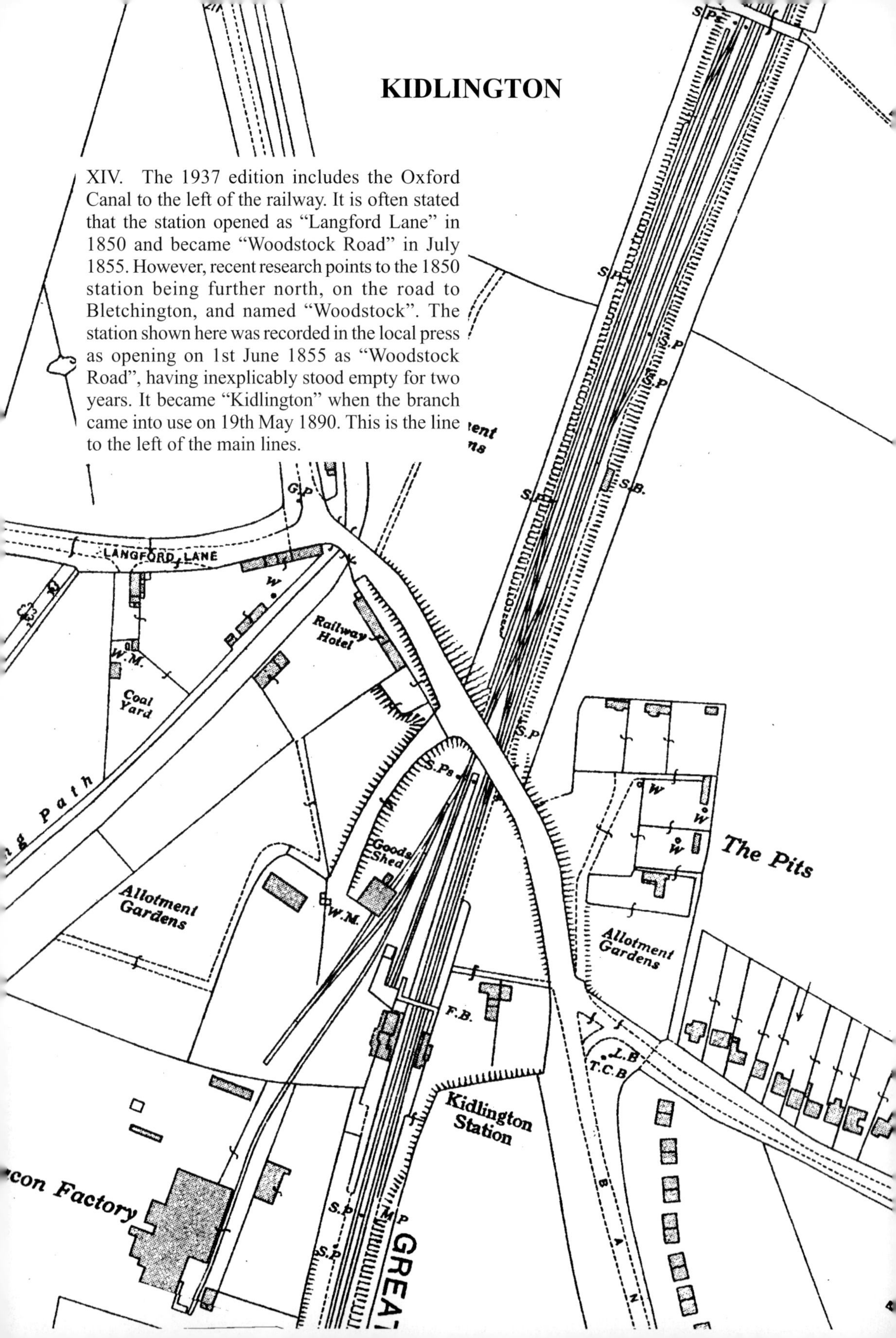

XIV. The 1937 edition includes the Oxford Canal to the left of the railway. It is often stated that the station opened as "Langford Lane" in 1850 and became "Woodstock Road" in July 1855. However, recent research points to the 1850 station being further north, on the road to Bletchington, and named "Woodstock". The station shown here was recorded in the local press as opening on 1st June 1855 as "Woodstock Road", having inexplicably stood empty for two years. It became "Kidlington" when the branch came into use on 19th May 1890. This is the line to the left of the main lines.

67. The branch train is in the bay platform, while a down stopping train disgorges its passengers, probably in the 1920s. There was a staff of 10 in that decade. Traffic was heavy during World War II, 22,373 tickets being issued in 1944 for example; by 1959, the figure was only 3217. Passenger services were withdrawn on 2nd November 1964 and the footbridge was removed for re-use near Didcot. (Lens of Sutton)

68. We now have two panoramas from June 1962. A lone van stands on the siding that was extended to the Oxfordshire Farmers Bacon Factory in November 1923. The line was used by C. & T.Harris (Calne) Ltd from 1930 until December 1966, although the goods yard closed on 1st March 1965. The goods shed opened a few years after the station and had a 30cwt crane. The track is off centre in the doorway, as it was built for broad gauge traffic. The shed was demolished in 1984. (P.J.Garland/R.S.Carpenter coll.)

Kidlington	1903	1913	1923	1933
Passenger tickets issued	15480	16537	13423	6880
Season tickets issued	*	*	88	10
Parcels forwarded	5740	5837	6353	5613
General goods forwarded (tons)	1951	1476	1311	264
Coal and coke received (tons)	53	33	46	245
Other minerals received (tons)	12	1326	286	1972
General goods received (tons)	1284	861	1369	830
Trucks of livestock handled	47	119	104	88

(* not available.)

69. The 51-lever signal box was in use from 1890 until 16th September 1968. Passing through the left arch is the down goods loop, which had been formed in 1942. Prior to that time, the line had been used exclusively by branch trains. (P.J.Garland/R.S.Carpenter coll.)

Blenheim & Woodstock Branch

70. The branch diverged from the main line one mile north of Kidlington, within sight of Bletchington Cement Works, which is visible in the distance. The branch closed completely on 1st March 1954, but remained in place until 1959. A wheel fractured on a down express in this vicinity on 24th December 1874, resulting in 34 fatalities. (R.M.Casserley)

SHIPTON-ON-CHERWELL HALT

71. This and the previous photograph date from March 1957. The halt opened on 1st April 1929 and served a community of about 100, nearly one mile distant. (R.M.Casserley)

XV. The map is from 1937.

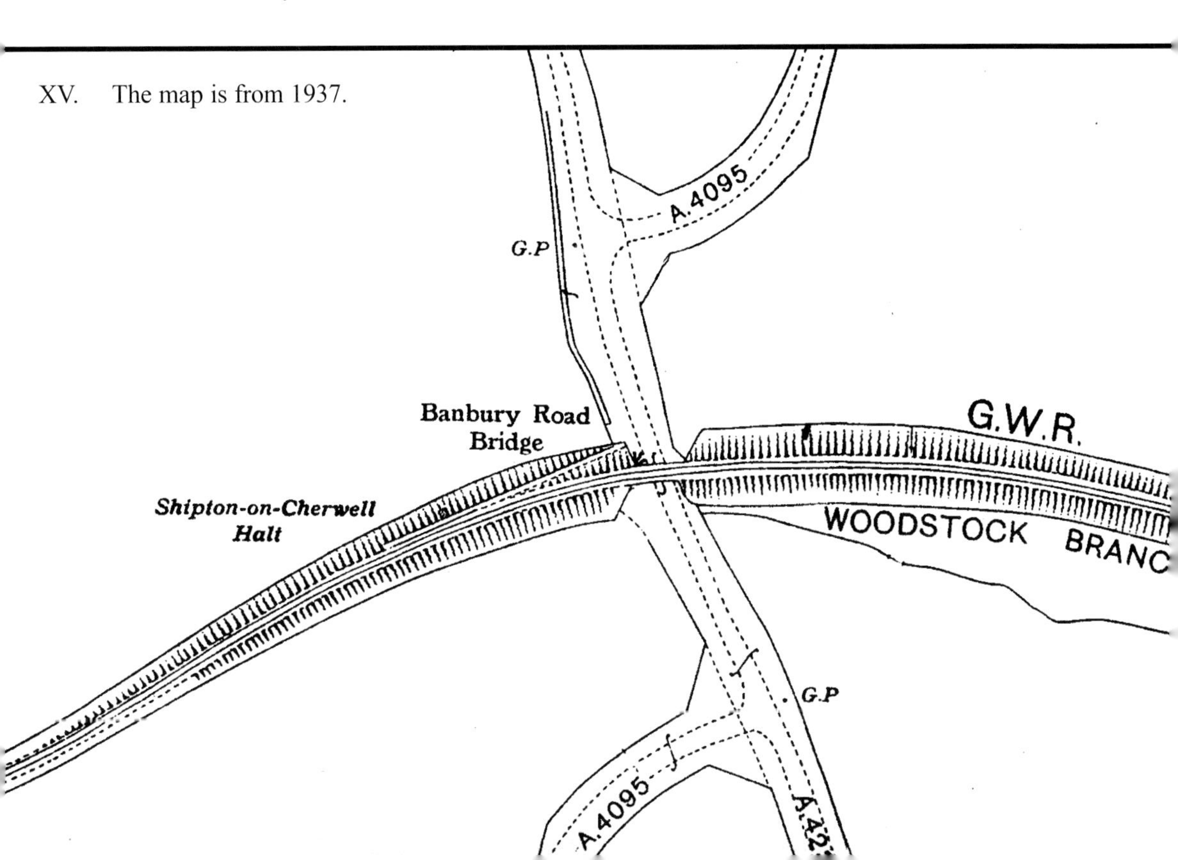

BLENHEIM & WOODSTOCK

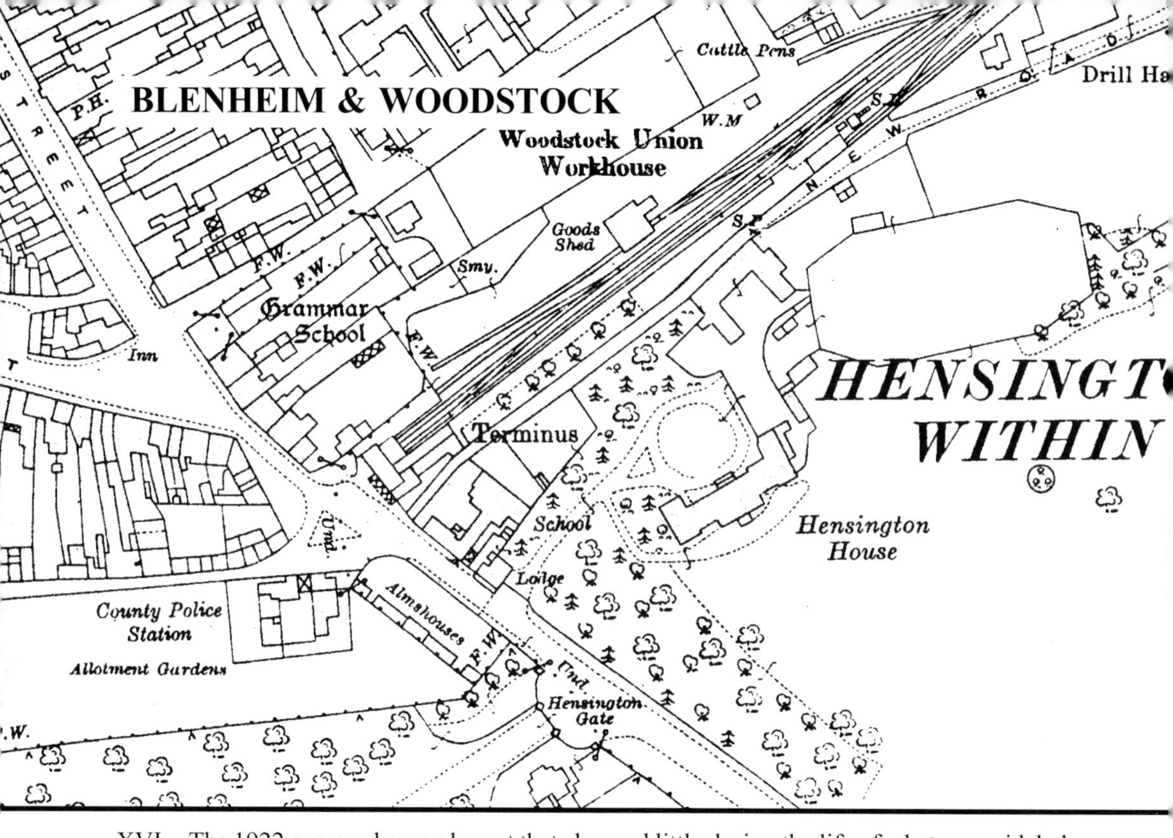

XVI. The 1922 survey shows a layout that changed little during the life of what was widely known as simply The Woodstock Branch. The town had a population of 1106 in 1901, but was a royal borough with a mayor and corporation. Nearby is the massive Blenheim Park, one of the many gates being at the bottom of the map. The great mansion was a gift from the nation to the first Duke of Marlborough, victor of Blenheim and other battles. The original palace was associated with the story of Lady Rosamund, the mistress of Henry VIII. There were many visits by nobility and royalty, royal trains appearing occasionally in the 1890s.

72. This postcard view includes the lofty wooden signal box, which was in use until 1926. The engine shed is to the right of it, this closing on 17th June 1927, by which time autotrains were employed universally on the branch. (Lens of Sutton)

73. The 4.53pm from Kidlington on 10th May 1930 was formed of autocoach no. 119 and 0-4-2T no. 1473 *Fair Rosamund* named after the famous mistress, but cut up in 1935. There was a staff of five here that year. (H.C.Casserley)

74. A 1949 photograph features trailer no. W58; 0-6-0PT no. 5413 was providing the power. The 5400 class was not used frequently on the branch, 0-4-2Ts being the usual motive power on the 3¾ mile long line. (J.Moss/R.S.Carpenter coll.)

75. Another 1949 view and this shows that the loop line had been removed by that time, but that the goods yard was still busy. One goods train each weekday sufficed. (J.Moss/R.S.Carpenter coll.)

76. This and the next picture were taken on the last day of operation, 27th February 1954. A large Vauxhall and a small Ford obstruct the view of the elegant building, which was converted to a garage. The town housed 1830 souls by 1961. (A.W.V.Mace/Milepost 92½ Picture Library)

77. The now preserved no. 1420 has *Fair Rosamund* chalked on its tank and raised eyes on its smokebox door. The coach on the left was attached to the front of the locomotive later that day. Goods traffic also ceased at that time. (R.S.Carpenter)

Blenheim and Woodstock	1903	1913	1923	1933
Passenger tickets issued	17436	17168	19117	23295
Season tickets issued	*	*	236	22
Parcels forwarded	14184	14943	11861	14279
General goods forwarded (tons)	744	1180	2482	620
Coal and coke received (tons)	427	753	420	540
Other minerals received (tons)	1695	1746	2017	1077
General goods received (tons)	1877	2295	2061	930
Trucks of livestock handled	128	242	85	29

(* not available.)

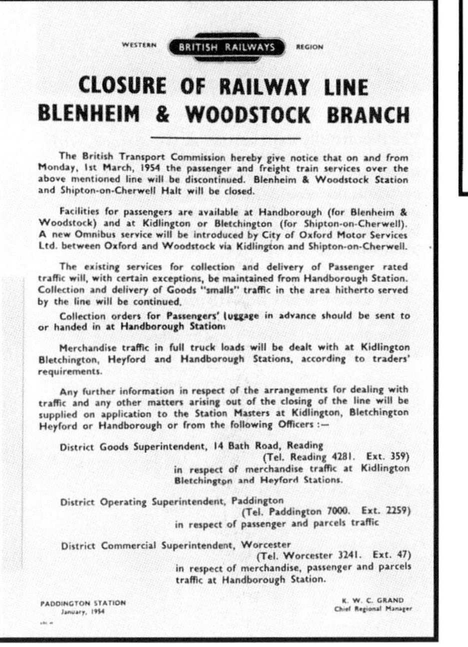

WESTERN BRITISH RAILWAYS REGION

CLOSURE OF RAILWAY LINE
BLENHEIM & WOODSTOCK BRANCH

The British Transport Commission hereby give notice that on and from Monday, 1st March, 1954 the passenger and freight train services over the above mentioned line will be discontinued. Blenheim & Woodstock Station and Shipton-on-Cherwell Halt will be closed.

Facilities for passengers are available at Handborough (for Blenheim & Woodstock) and at Kidlington or Bletchington (for Shipton-on-Cherwell). A new Omnibus service will be introduced by City of Oxford Motor Services Ltd. between Oxford and Woodstock via Kidlington and Shipton-on-Cherwell.

The existing services for collection and delivery of Passenger rated traffic will, with certain exceptions, be maintained from Handborough Station. Collection and delivery of Goods "smalls" traffic in the area hitherto served by the line will be continued.

Collection orders for Passengers' Luggage in advance should be sent to or handed in at Handborough Station.

Merchandise traffic in full truck loads will be dealt with at Kidlington Bletchington, Heyford and Handborough Stations, according to traders' requirements.

Any further information in respect of the arrangements for dealing with traffic and any other matters arising out of the closing of the line will be supplied on application to the Station Masters at Kidlington, Bletchington Heyford or Handborough or from the following Officers :—

District Goods Superintendent, 14 Bath Road, Reading
(Tel. Reading 4281. Ext. 359)
in respect of merchandise traffic at Kidlington Bletchington and Heyford Stations.

District Operating Superintendent, Paddington
(Tel. Paddington 7000. Ext. 2259)
in respect of passenger and parcels traffic

District Commercial Superintendent, Worcester
(Tel. Worcester 3241. Ext. 47)
in respect of merchandise, passenger and parcels traffic at Handborough Station.

PADDINGTON STATION
January, 1954

K. W. C. GRAND
Chief Regional Manager

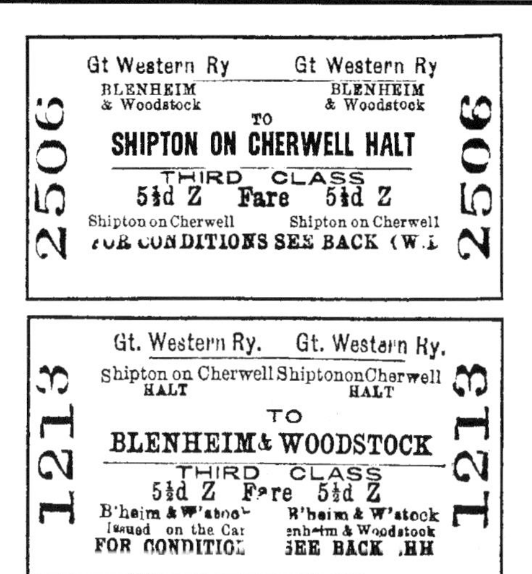

SOUTH OF BLETCHINGTON

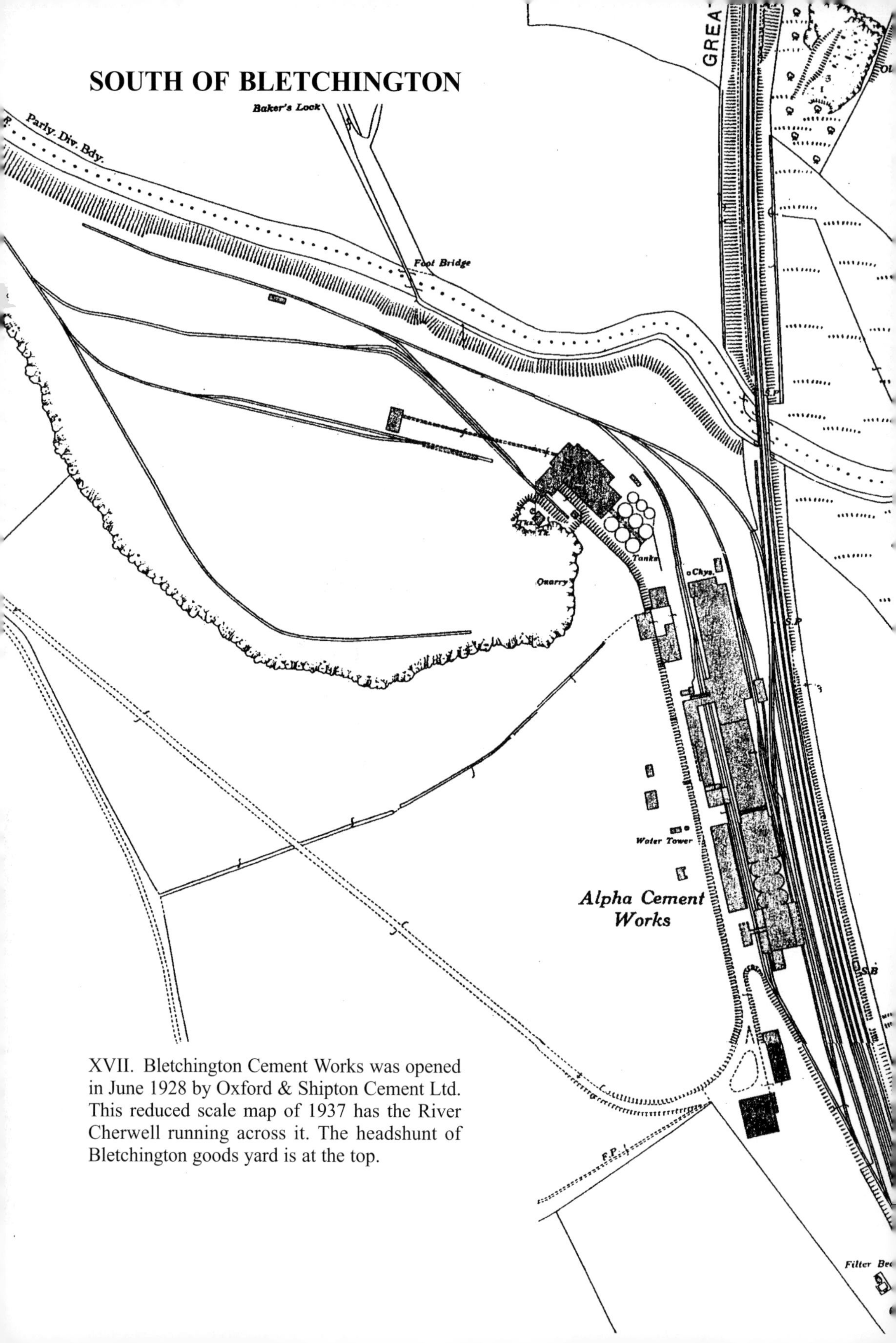

XVII. Bletchington Cement Works was opened in June 1928 by Oxford & Shipton Cement Ltd. This reduced scale map of 1937 has the River Cherwell running across it. The headshunt of Bletchington goods yard is at the top.

78. APCM Ltd owned the works when their Bagnall no. 2 of 1921 was photographed on 20th March 1968. The signal box had 24 levers and was in use from 7th November 1927 until 16th September 1968. (M.A.N.Johnston)

BLETCHINGTON

79. A short siding was provided on the up side to serve the cattle dock (centre). The goods line passed behind the down platform and its small shelter. There is a small crane beyond the unusual goods shed. (LGRP/NRM)

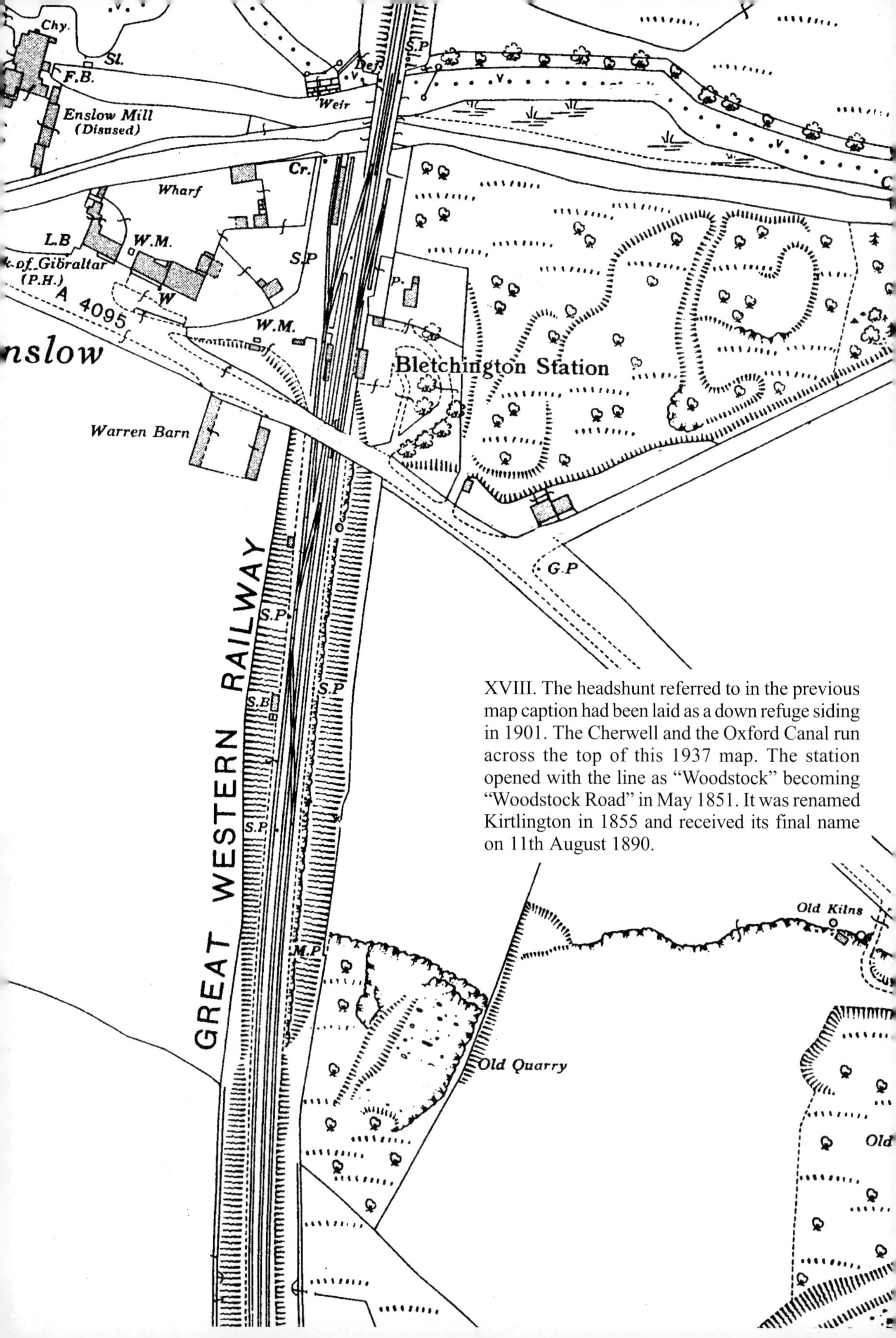

XVIII. The headshunt referred to in the previous map caption had been laid as a down refuge siding in 1901. The Cherwell and the Oxford Canal run across the top of this 1937 map. The station opened with the line as "Woodstock" becoming "Woodstock Road" in May 1851. It was renamed Kirtlington in 1855 and received its final name on 11th August 1890.

80. The up side is viewed from a down train in March 1955. The long down siding is evident through the bridge arch. The cement works is in the distance. There were 11 or 12 men working here in the 1930s. (R.M.Casserley)

81. Another southward view and this includes the 29-lever signal box that was functioning from about 1914 until 23rd April 1967. Passenger traffic ceased here on 2nd November 1964 and goods followed on 21st June 1965. (Lens of Sutton coll.)

Bletchington	1903	1913	1923	1933
Passenger tickets issued	11051	11334	8191	13652
Season tickets issued	*	26	101	55
Parcels forwarded	9580	13190	7265	3146
General goods forwarded (tons)	1042	9114	10249	129396
Coal and coke received (tons)	84	70	75	199
Other minerals received (tons)	270	289	554	7748
General goods received (tons)	2288	2597	2044	1310
Trucks of livestock handled	151	94	90	80

(* not available.)

TACKLEY

82. Tackley Halt was opened on 6th April 1931 and was photographed in October 1957. It seems that there was a shortage of Pagoda shelters in 1931. Tackley signal box was in use from 1901 to 1950 and was ¼ mile to the north. The term halt was dropped on 5th March 1961. (R.M.Casserley)

83. Unlike most other halts, this was a success and was still in use on 25th April 2002 when photographed as a class 168 "Countryman" of Chiltern Trains sped through. Normally these units did not work on this route. Services on the Marylebone to Birmingham line were diverted out of Paddington at this time, while the Bicester to Banbury section was doubled. The level crossing at Tackley serves a farm. It is the end of the road through the village. (M.Turvey)

84. Virgin Cross-Country Trains Voyager no. 220016 was bound for Bournemouth on the same day. These high per-formance trains have a diesel-electric unit in each coach. The tilting version began trials on this route later that year. Their bogies are slightly different but the body tilt is only eight degrees. (M.Turvey)

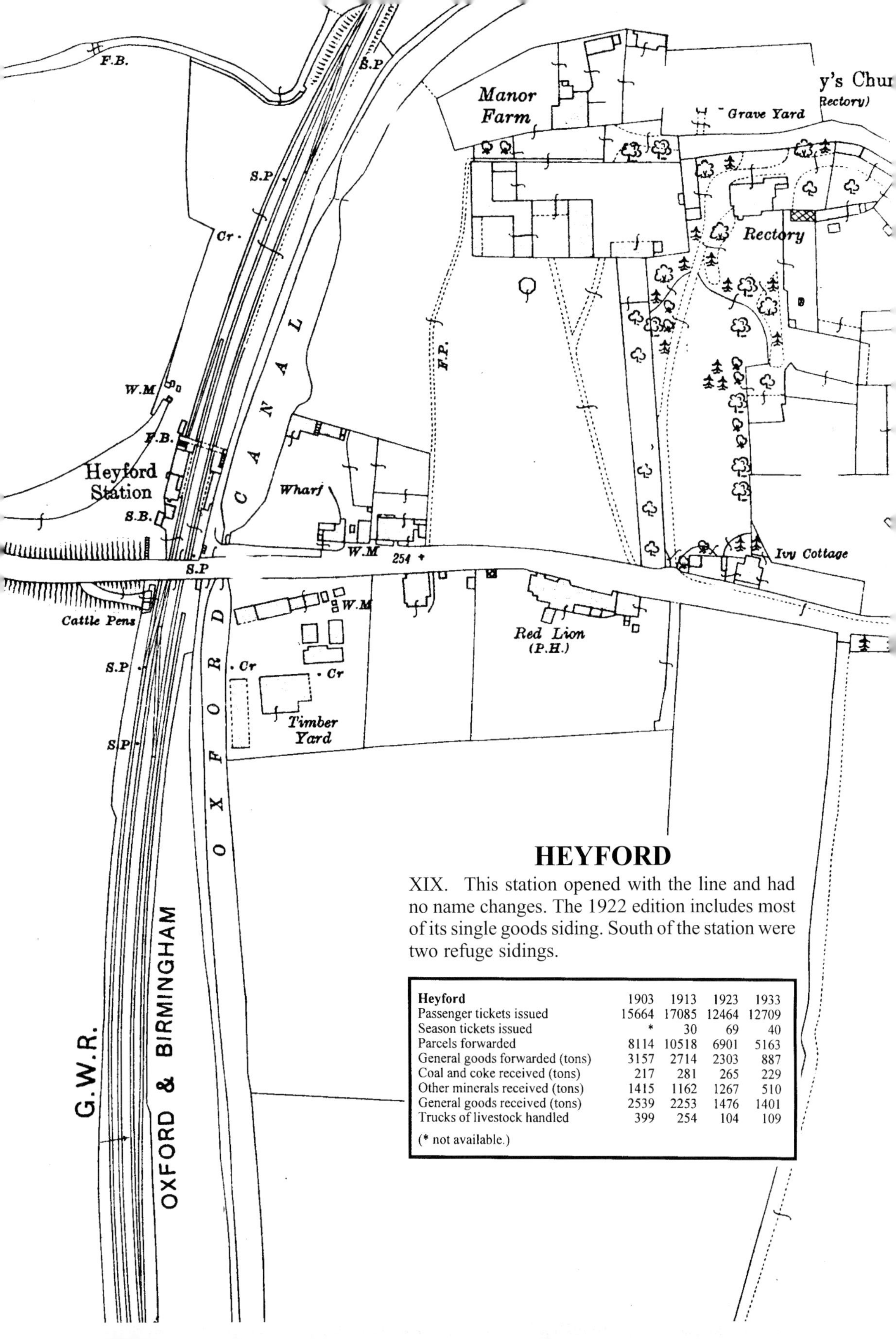

HEYFORD

XIX. This station opened with the line and had no name changes. The 1922 edition includes most of its single goods siding. South of the station were two refuge sidings.

Heyford	1903	1913	1923	1933
Passenger tickets issued	15664	17085	12464	12709
Season tickets issued	*	30	69	40
Parcels forwarded	8114	10518	6901	5163
General goods forwarded (tons)	3157	2714	2303	887
Coal and coke received (tons)	217	281	265	229
Other minerals received (tons)	1415	1162	1267	510
General goods received (tons)	2539	2253	1476	1401
Trucks of livestock handled	399	254	104	109

(* not available.)

85. This northward view features the wide track spacing resulting from the line having been broad gauge initially. The signal box had 22 levers and was functional until 16th September 1968. (LGRP/NRM)

86. A southward view in July 1958 includes the siding, which was in use until 24th May 1965. It was the location of a collision between a down express and a locomotive shunting on 26th November 1852. The driver of the fast train died. (H.C.Casserley)

87. The finely detailed limestone structure was destroyed by official vandals sometime after this photograph was taken in 1958. There were seven or eight employees here in the 1930s. (H.C.Casserley)

88. No buildings remained when Thames Turbo no. 166213 called to pick up a passenger on 25th April 2002. Railway observers are recommended to hire a boat here as the railway and waterway are in close proximity for many miles. (M.Turvey)

FRITWELL AND SOMERTON

XX. Opened with the line as "Somerton", the station was renamed "Somerton (Oxon)" in 1906 following the opening of Somerton in Somerset. Its final name was adopted on 1st October 1907. The 1922 map includes a length of Oxford Canal and the single siding. The crane (Cr.) was rated at 30cwt.

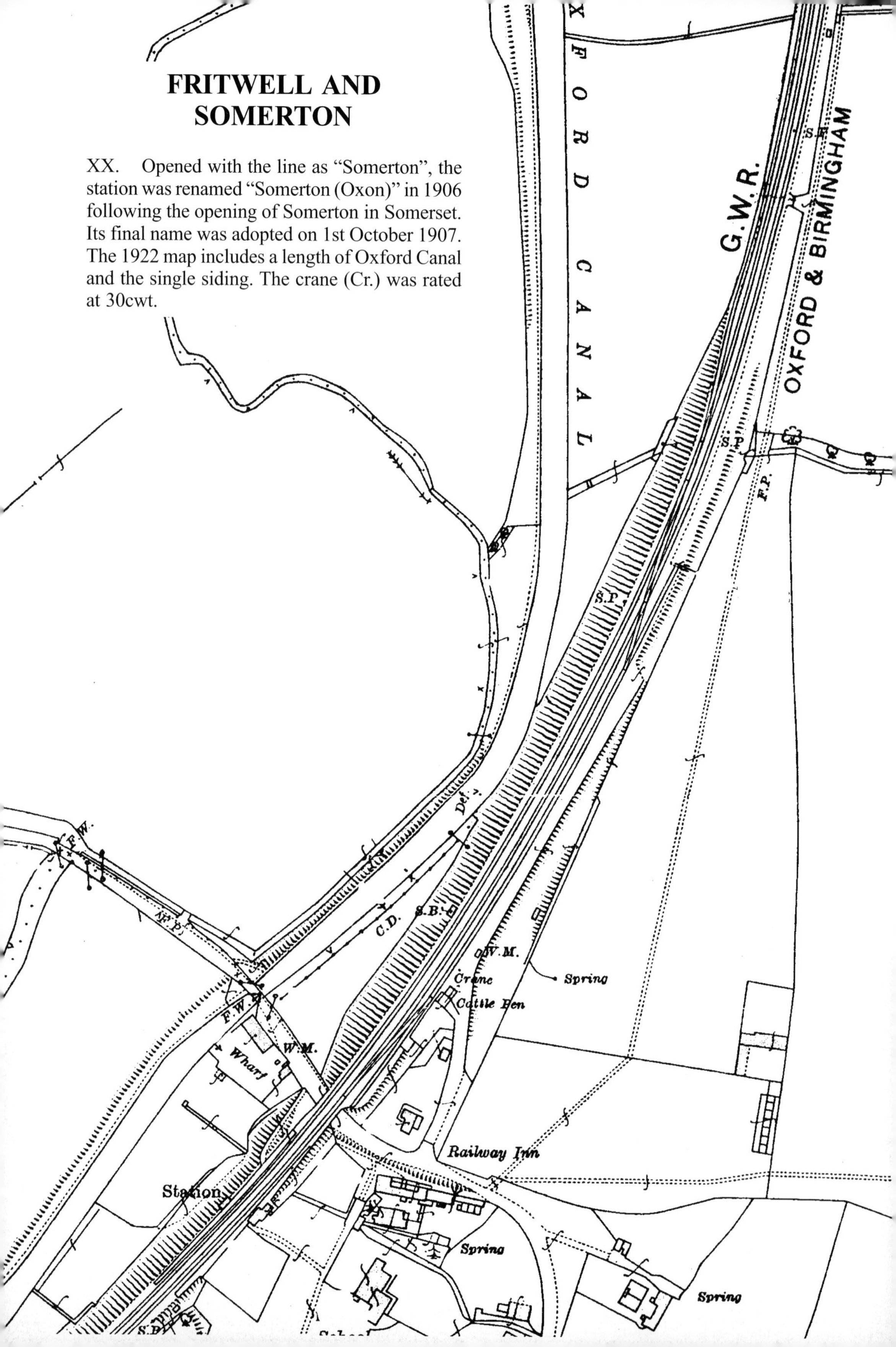

89. This postcard includes the 1906-07 name and the cattle dock. We are looking towards Banbury. The signal box is out of view, on the left. It had 28 levers and was open from 1880 to 1966. Five or six men were employed here until at least 1938. (Lens of Sutton)

Fritwell and Somerton	1903	1913	1923	1933
Passenger tickets issued	7234	8073	7096	6880
Season tickets issued	*	4	82	21
Parcels forwarded	6056	11101	6304	3028
General goods forwarded (tons)	1580	1131	1183	309
Coal and coke received (tons)	45	126	99	157
Other minerals received (tons)	770	1252	1209	172
General goods received (tons)	1248	1617	721	210
Trucks of livestock handled	103	135	79	79

(* not available.)

90. A southward view in 1962 includes a set of portable steps for use on the exceptionally low platforms. Passenger service was withdrawn on 4th May 1964 and goods traffic ceased on 2nd November of that year. (P.J.Garland/R.S.Carpenter coll.)

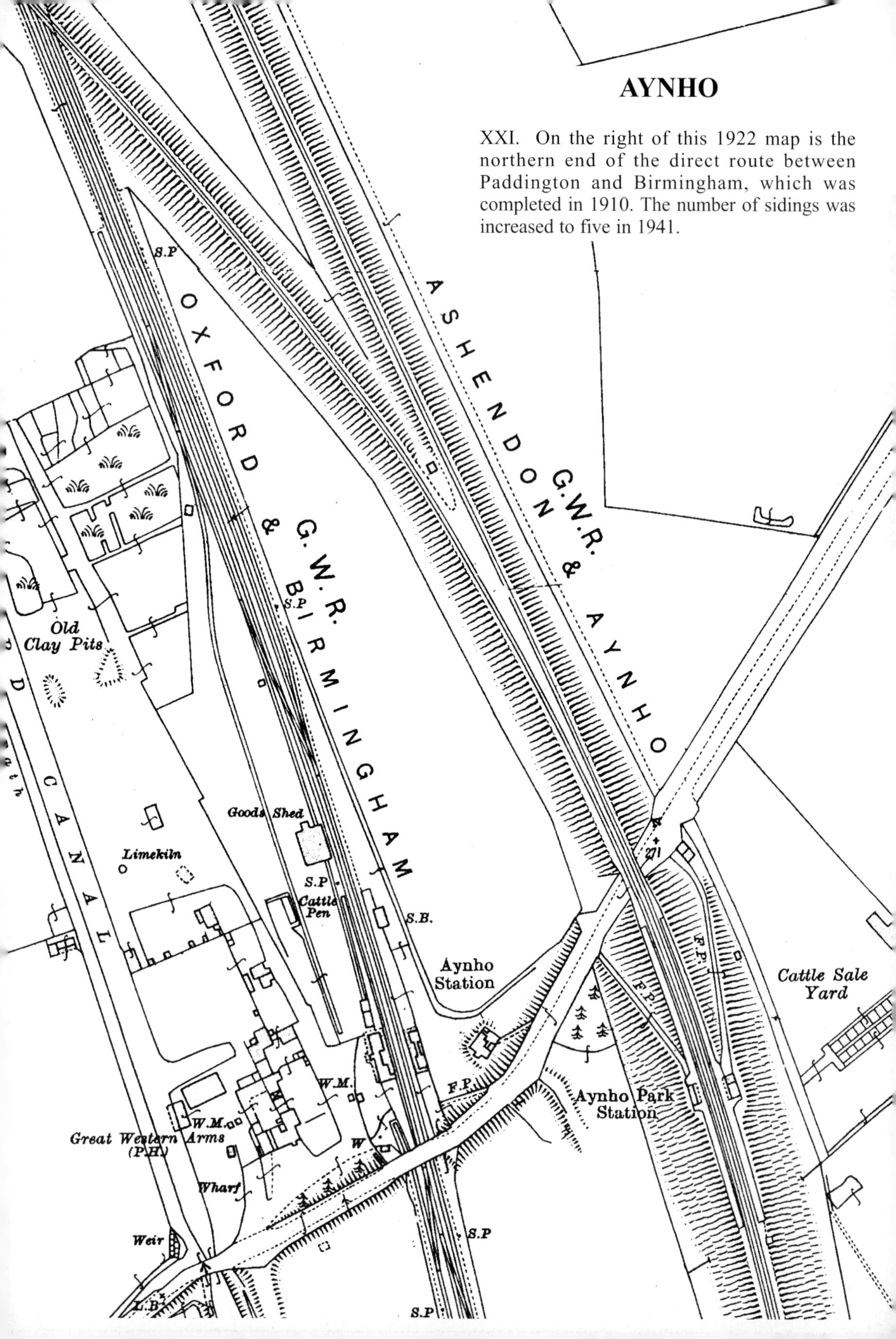

AYNHO

XXI. On the right of this 1922 map is the northern end of the direct route between Paddington and Birmingham, which was completed in 1910. The number of sidings was increased to five in 1941.

91. This was the third of the 1850 intermediate stations; all were of similar plan. A memorable accident took place on the day before the route was extended to Birmingham. The ceremonial train, with Brunel and Gooch on the footplate of 4-2-2 *Lord of the Isles*, crashed into wagons being shunted. The locomotive lost its front wheels, the officials lost their dignity and lunch was late. (LGRP/NRM)

92. Two photographs from 8th June 1939 emphasise the importance of the route as a freight artery. Empties return north behind 0-6-0 no. 2295 and pass the down refuge siding. This was a loop between 1915 and 1963 and was removed in 1964. The 1910 route is in the background of this and the previous photograph. (H.C.Casserley)

93. With a good clear exhaust, 2-8-0 no. 2875 hauls its loaded wagons passed the 31-lever signal box, which was functional from about 1900 to 16th September 1968. The staff level was 9 to 12 in the 1930s. (H.C.Casserley)

→

94. The station closed to goods on 4th May 1964 and to passengers on 2nd November following. It is seen on 23rd July 1988 as no. 47466 passes with the 06.40 Manchester Piccadilly to Portsmouth Harbour via Guildford, a Saturdays-only service. (P.G.Barnes)

Aynho	1903	1913	1923	1933
Passenger tickets issued	12406	13153	11338	9947
Season tickets issued	*	55	83	50
Parcels forwarded	5187	7982	6897	4321
General goods forwarded (tons)	1419	1617	1342	140
Coal and coke received (tons)	93	103	46	114
Other minerals received (tons)	212	771	4413	225
General goods received (tons)	1957	1451	1403	433
Trucks of livestock handled	244	159	160	31

(* not available.)

→

95. Having just passed the 1912 up loop, no. 47450 accelerates south on 21st July 1989 attached to DVT 82118. The train had been scheduled to arrive at Euston, but was diverted due to a derailment at Harrow. The loop and station building were still extant in 2002. (M.Turvey)

Aynho Park Halt is illustrated in
***Princes Risborough to Banbury* (Middleton Press).**

NORTH OF AYNHO

96. The flood plain of the Cherwell Valley is on the right as we look south at the 1910 junction. (LGRP/NRM)

97. Devoid of smoke deflectors, ex-SR 4-6-0 no. 777 *Sir Lamiel* joins the 1850 route on the 6th July 1986, while working the "Shakespeare Limited" from Marylebone to Stratford-upon-Avon. The signal box was taken out of use on 2nd April 1992, but remained standing until July 2002. (S.P.Derek)

98. Approaching Aynho Junction with coal for Didcot Power Station on 27th April 1991 is no. 58032. This traffic diminished later that decade as much of Didcot's coal was subsequently imported via Avonmouth. There were water troughs in this vicinity until 1967. (B.Morrison)

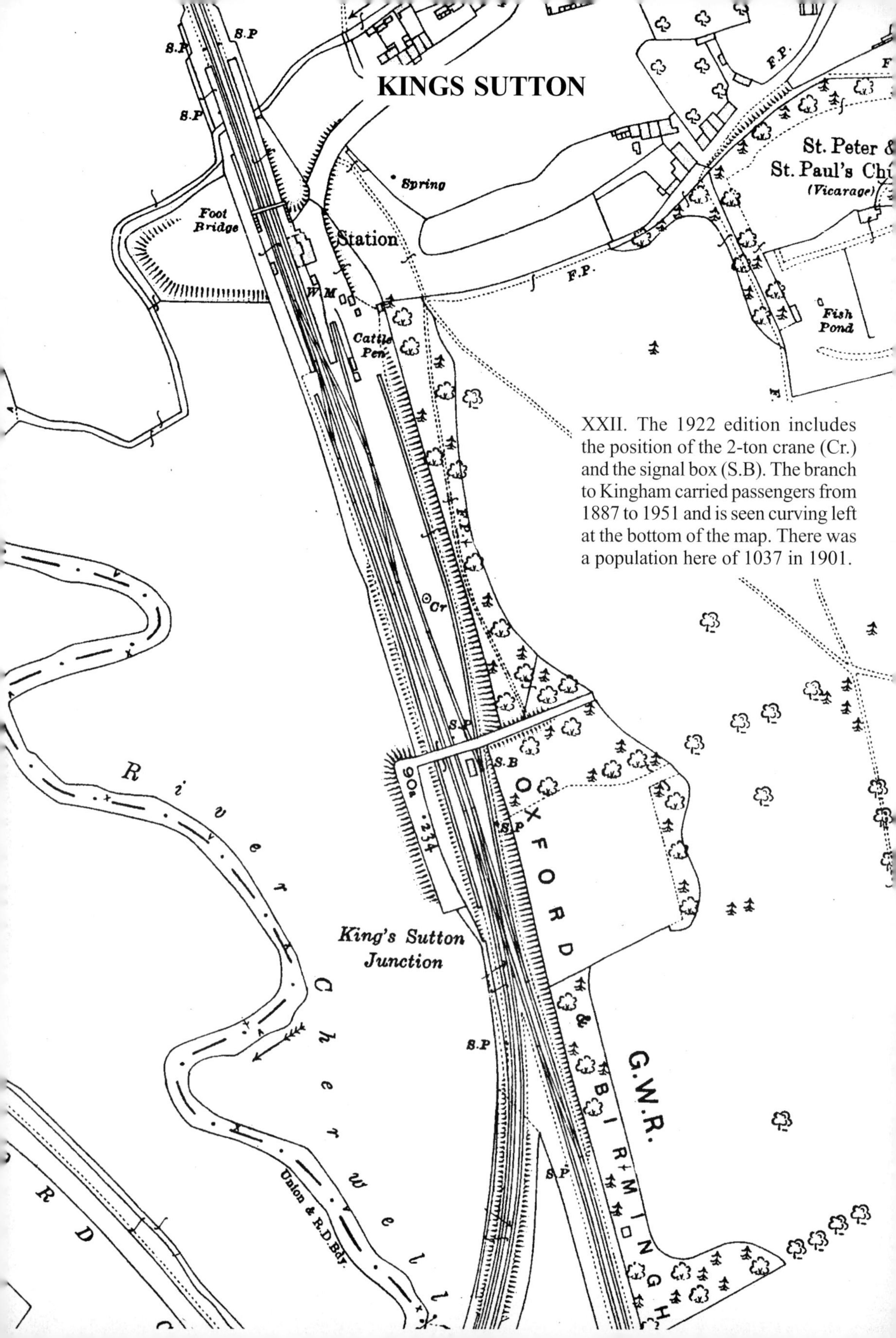

XXII. The 1922 edition includes the position of the 2-ton crane (Cr.) and the signal box (S.B). The branch to Kingham carried passengers from 1887 to 1951 and is seen curving left at the bottom of the map. There was a population here of 1037 in 1901.

99. The locomotive appears to be no. 4953 *Pitchford Hall* and it is working an Oxford to Banbury service in the early 1930s. The Kingham route (right) was retained for a short distance as a single siding until 1971. (R.S.Carpenter coll.)

100. No. 3338 *Swift* was recorded with a Banbury to Oxford service, but the date was not. The siding in the foreground received yellow ochre via a tramway from Adderbury Pits until about 1900. There was a staff of 10 or 11 between the wars. (LGRP/NRM)

101. A southward view from the early 1960s includes the 39-lever signal box, which was in use from 1887 until 4th April 1971. Kings Sutton was designated a halt from 2nd November 1964 until 6th May 1968. (Lens of Sutton Coll.)

102. DMU no. 207 was working the 17.12 Banbury to Oxford service on 23rd July 1988. Note that the footbridge had been replaced by a crossing, despite the dangerous bend. (P.G.Barnes)

103. No. 165029 was forming the 09.40 Marylebone to Banbury on 25th September 1993. Chiltern Trains subsequently greatly enhanced the service at this station and Thames Trains Oxford services continued to call a few times on weekdays. (P.G.Barnes)

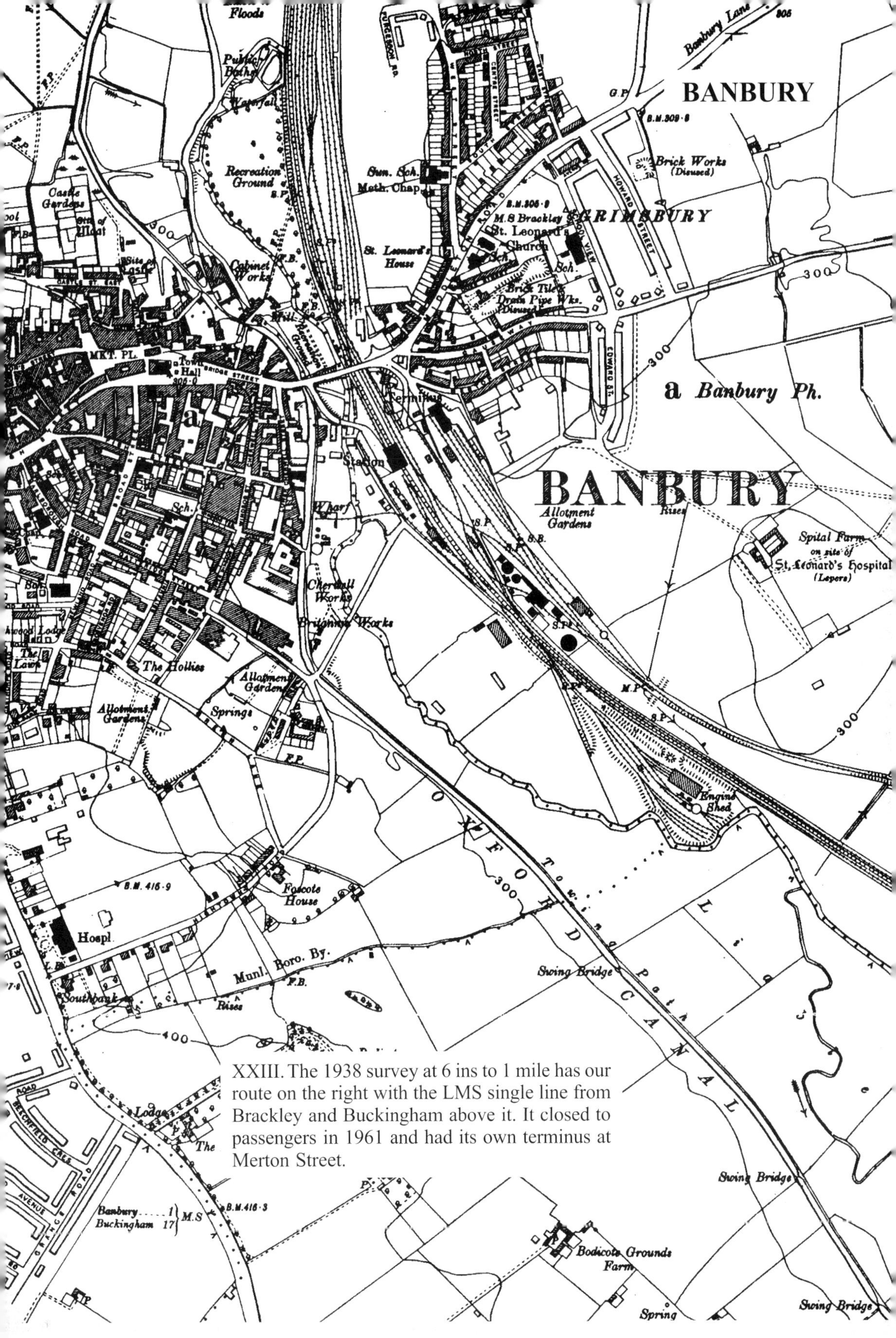

XXIII. The 1938 survey at 6 ins to 1 mile has our route on the right with the LMS single line from Brackley and Buckingham above it. It closed to passengers in 1961 and had its own terminus at Merton Street.

104. A southward view in 1932 features the overall roof and its associated lofty chimneys. The goods shed is beyond. Reconstruction was planned in 1938, but delayed by the war. Despite bays having been added in 1903, the station was often very congested. (LGRP/NRM)

105. No. 2914 *St Augustine* approaches the down platform on 11th September 1937 and is seen from the longer up platform. South Box is visible near the rear of the train. There were 210 employed here that year, excluding shed staff and footplatemen. (H.C.Casserley)

106. The overall roof was removed in 1952 for safety reasons and the platforms were made to be of equal length at the south end soon after. Ex-LMS class 5 4-6-0 no. 45493 runs in with a northbound express. (Rev.J.Parker)

107. The station was completely rebuilt in 1956-58, in concrete. The 1.8 pm from Oxford has just arrived on 25th August 1960, hauled by 2-6-2T no.4125. (M.Mensing/M.J.Stretton coll)

108. Banbury has for long had trains between a large number of stations in the north and south. No. 34061 *73 Squadron* is heading a Leeds to Poole train on 27th July 1963; there would be steam haulage for another three years. (D.Trevor Rowe)

109. Following the lifting of the steam ban, Banbury drew the crowds on a number of occasions. The GWS fielded no. 7808 *Cookham Manor* and no. 6998 *Burton Agnes Hall* on 19th October 1974 for a Didcot to Stratford-on-Avon trip. The extent of the rebuilt station is evident. (T.Heavyside)

7808

110. An empty Merry-go-round coal train from Didcot was recorded near South Box on 1st October 1975, hauled by no. 47326. Clocks on posts were an innovative feature of the rebuilt station. (T.Heavyside)

111. South Box was still working semaphore signals in 2003. This panel had been added in 1992 to control the Aynho Junction area. This meant that the number of levers had to be reduced from 87 to 65 to accommodate it. (L.Crosier)

112. The crowds were out again on 12th October 1986 to witness the presence of speed record holder no. 4468 *Mallard*. It stopped for water while working the "Shakespeare Limited" from Marylebone to Stratford-upon-Avon. (S.P.Derek)

Other views of this station can be found in *Princes Risborough to Banbury* (Middleton Press).

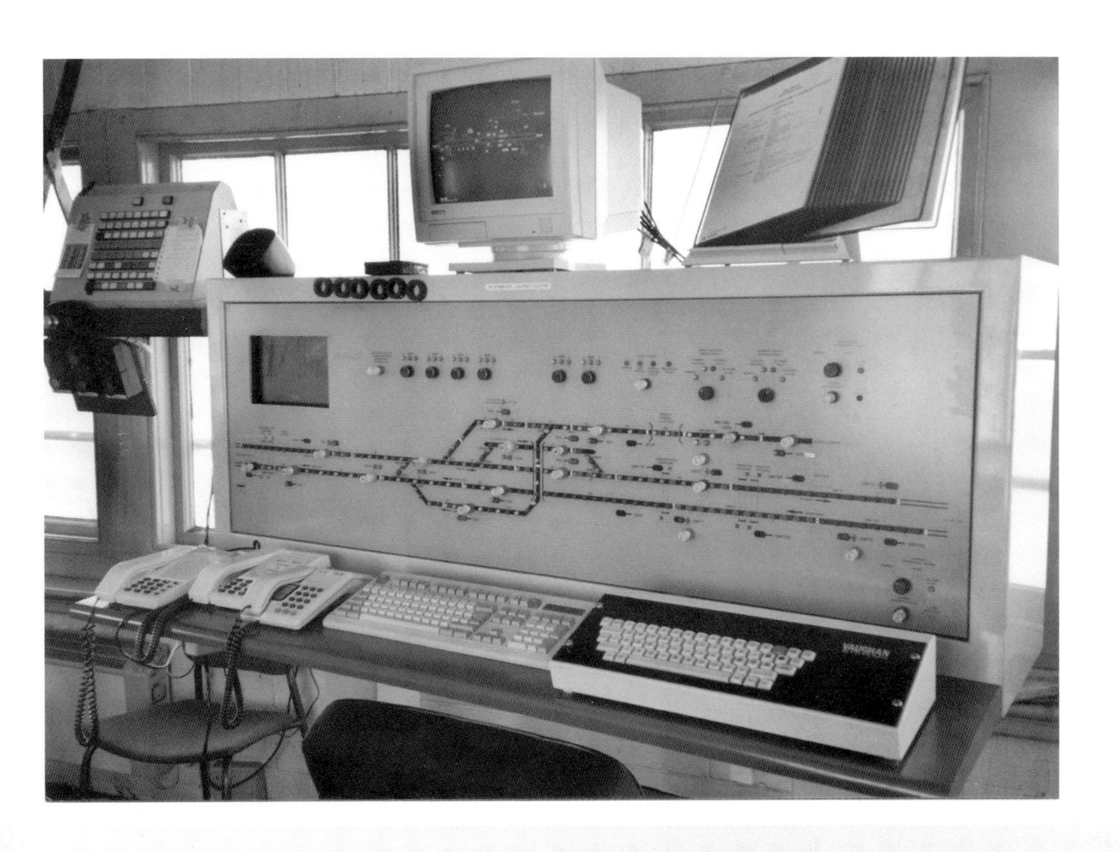
VAUGHAN

BANBURY STATION
No 4468

113. On the left of this northward view is platform 1, which serves the down relief line. At platform 3 on 9th March 1996 is Thames Turbo no. 165133 working the 13.45 Banbury to Paddington service. On the the right is a bay platform (no.4), which was once the haunt of the Princes Risborough autotrain. (P.G.Barnes)

114. At the north end is a bay devoid of a number in which a rescue locomotive often stands. The "Thunderbird" on 11th June 2002 was no. 47726 *Progress*. Passing through platform 3 were nos. 65532 and 66501. (V.Mitchell)

BANBURY SHED

115. Heavy lifting equipment was available near the 1908 shed, which was south of the station. Seen on the 11th September 1937 is no. 3005, one of the Railway Operating Department's 2-8-0s built for war work, but not introduced until 1919. (H.C.Casserley)

116. Loading after a shed visit on 29th October 1950, is diesel railcar no.14, one of the first batch of AEC-engined cars. It was completed in 1936 and had 70 seats. There were 79 locomotives allocated here in 1948, but only 64 in 1950 and 35 in 1960. (R.J.Buckley/Initial Photographics)

117. Also recorded in the early 1950s was no. 3216, one of the 2251 class, introduced in 1930. Like some of its inmates, the ash shed was in terminal decline. The first engine shed had been a temporary affair in the 1850s. A brick-built one was erected in 1889 and a 45ft turntable was provided. Both lasted until 1908. (J.H.Moss/ R.S.Carpenter coll.)

118. The depot covered a large area and included a 65ft turntable (centre) and a coaling stage (left) similar to the one that can still be seen at the Didcot Railway Centre. (M.J.Stretton coll)

119. A panorama from 7th May 1966 includes five class 9F 2-10-0s, used on the ex-GCR route to Woodford Halse, and three ex-LMS class 5 4-6-0s. (G.P.Cooper)

120. The interior of a live-steam shed has a unique and indescribable atmosphere. Seen on 31st May 1966 were nos 92228 and 44710. The shed closed on 3rd October 1966, but the ambiance can still be enjoyed at Didcot on certain occasions. (R.S.Carpenter)

Easebourne Lane, Midhurst, W Sussex. GU29 9AZ Tel: 01730 813169 Fax: 01730 812601
Email: enquiries@middletonpress.fsnet.co.uk *If books are not available from your local transport stockist, order direct with cheque, Visa or Mastercard, post free UK.*

BRANCH LINES
Branch Line to Allhallows
Branch Line to Alton
Branch Lines around Ascot
Branch Line to Ashburton
Branch Lines around Bodmin
Branch Line to Bude
Branch Lines around Canterbury
Branch Lines around Chard & Yeovil
Branch Line to Cheddar
Branch Lines around Cromer
Branch Lines to East Grinstead
Branch Lines of East London
Branch Lines to Effingham Junction
Branch Lines around Exmouth
Branch Lines to Falmouth, Helston & St. Ives
Branch Line to Fairford
Branch Lines around Gosport
Branch Line to Hayling
Branch Lines to Henley, Windsor & Marlow
Branch Line to Hawkhurst
Branch Lines around Huntingdon
Branch Line to Ilfracombe
Branch Line to Kingsbridge
Branch Line to Kingswear
Branch Line to Lambourn
Branch Lines to Launceston & Princetown
Branch Lines to Longmoor
Branch Line to Looe
Branch Line to Lyme Regis
Branch Lines around Midhurst
Branch Line to Minehead
Branch Line to Moretonhampstead
Branch Lines to Newport (IOW)
Branch Lines to Newquay
Branch Lines around North Woolwich
Branch Line to Padstow
Branch Lines around Plymouth
Branch Lines to Seaton and Sidmouth
Branch Lines around Sheerness
Branch Line to Shrewsbury
Branch Line to Swanage *updated*
Branch Line to Tenterden
Branch Lines around Tiverton
Branch Lines to Torrington
Branch Line to Upwell
Branch Lines of West London
Branch Lines around Weymouth
Branch Lines around Wimborne
Branch Lines around Wisbech

NARROW GAUGE
Branch Line to Lynton
Branch Lines around Portmadoc 1923-46
Branch Lines around Porthmadog 1954-94
Branch Line to Southwold
Douglas to Port Erin
Douglas to Peel
Kent Narrow Gauge
Northern France Narrow Gauge
Romneyrail
Southern France Narrow Gauge
Sussex Narrow Gauge
Surrey Narrow Gauge
Two-Foot Gauge Survivors
Vivarais Narrow Gauge

SOUTH COAST RAILWAYS
Ashford to Dover
Bournemouth to Weymouth
Brighton to Worthing
Eastbourne to Hastings
Hastings to Ashford
Portsmouth to Southampton
Ryde to Ventnor
Southampton to Bournemouth

SOUTHERN MAIN LINES
Basingstoke to Salisbury
Bromley South to Rochester
Crawley to Littlehampton
Dartford to Sittingbourne
East Croydon to Three Bridges
Epsom to Horsham
Exeter to Barnstaple
Exeter to Tavistock
Faversham to Dover
London Bridge to East Croydon
Orpington to Tonbridge
Tonbridge to Hastings
Salisbury to Yeovil
Sittingbourne to Ramsgate
Swanley to Ashford
Tavistock to Plymouth
Three Bridges to Brighton
Victoria to Bromley South
Victoria to East Croydon
Waterloo to Windsor
Waterloo to Woking
Woking to Portsmouth
Woking to Southampton
Yeovil to Exeter

EASTERN MAIN LINES
Barking to Southend
Ely to Kings Lynn
Ely to Norwich
Fenchurch Street to Barking
Ilford to Shenfield
Ipswich to Saxmundham
Liverpool Street to Ilford
Saxmundham to Yarmouth
Tilbury Loop

WESTERN MAIN LINES
Didcot to Banbury
Didcot to Swindon
Ealing to Slough
Exeter to Newton Abbot
Newton Abbot to Plymouth
Newbury to Westbury
Paddington to Ealing
Paddington to Princes Risborough
Plymouth to St. Austell
Princes Risborough to Banbury
Reading to Didcot
Slough to Newbury
St. Austell to Penzance
Swindon to Bristol
Taunton to Exeter
Westbury to Taunton

MIDLAND MAIN LINES
Euston to Harrow & Wealdstone
St. Pancras to St. Albans

COUNTRY RAILWAY ROUTES
Abergavenny to Merthyr
Andover to Southampton
Bath to Evercreech Junction
Bath Green Park to Bristol
Burnham to Evercreech Junction
Cheltenham to Andover
Croydon to East Grinstead
Didcot to Winchester
East Kent Light Railway
Fareham to Salisbury
Guildford to Redhill
Reading to Basingstoke
Reading to Guildford
Redhill to Ashford
Salisbury to Westbury
Stratford upon Avon to Cheltenham
Strood to Paddock Wood
Taunton to Barnstaple
Wenford Bridge to Fowey
Westbury to Bath
Woking to Alton
Yeovil to Dorchester

GREAT RAILWAY ERAS
Ashford from Steam to Eurostar
Clapham Junction 50 years of change
Festiniog in the Fifties
Festiniog in the Sixties
Festiniog 50 years of enterprise
Isle of Wight Lines 50 years of change
Railways to Victory 1944-46
Return to Blaenau 1970-82
SECR Centenary album
Talyllyn 50 years of change
Yeovil 50 years of change

LONDON SUBURBAN RAILWAYS
Caterham and Tattenham Corner
Charing Cross to Dartford
Clapham Jn. to Beckenham Jn.
Crystal Palace (HL) & Catford Loop
East London Line
Finsbury Park to Alexandra Palace
Holbourn Viaduct to Lewisham
Kingston and Hounslow Loops
Lewisham to Dartford
Lines around Wimbledon
Liverpool Street to Chingford
London Bridge to Addiscombe
Mitcham Junction Lines
North London Line
South London Line
West Croydon to Epsom
West London Line
Willesden Junction to Richmond
Wimbledon to Beckenham
Wimbledon to Epsom

STEAMING THROUGH
Steaming through Cornwall
Steaming through the Isle of Wight
Steaming through Kent
Steaming through West Hants

TRAMWAY CLASSICS
Aldgate & Stepney Tramways
Barnet & Finchley Tramways
Bath Tramways
Brighton's Tramways
Bristol's Tramways
Burton & Ashby Tramways
Camberwell & W.Norwood Tramways
Clapham & Streatham Tramways
Croydon's Tramways
Dover's Tramways
East Ham & West Ham Tramways
Edgware and Willesden Tramways
Eltham & Woolwich Tramways
Embankment & Waterloo Tramways
Enfield & Wood Green Tramways
Exeter & Taunton Tramways
Greenwich & Dartford Tramways
Hammersmith & Hounslow Tramways
Hampstead & Highgate Tramways
Hastings Tramways
Holborn & Finsbury Tramways
Ilford & Barking Tramways
Kingston & Wimbledon Tramways
Lewisham & Catford Tramways
Liverpool Tramways 1. Eastern Routes
Liverpool Tramways 2. Southern Routes
Liverpool Tramways 3. Northern Routes
Maidstone & Chatham Tramways
Margate to Ramsgate
North Kent Tramways
Norwich Tramways
Reading Tramways
Seaton & Eastbourne Tramways
Shepherds Bush & Uxbridge Tramways
Southend-on-sea Tramways
Southwark & Deptford Tramways
Stamford Hill Tramways
Twickenham & Kingston Tramways
Victoria & Lambeth Tramways
Waltham Cross & Edmonton Tramways
Walthamstow & Leyton Tramways
Wandsworth & Battersea Tramways

TROLLEYBUS CLASSICS
Croydon Trolleybuses
Derby Trolleybuses
Hastings Trolleybuses
Huddersfield Trolleybuses
Maidstone Trolleybuses
Portsmouth Trolleybuses
Woolwich & Dartford Trolleybuses

WATERWAY ALBUMS
Kent and East Sussex Waterways
London to Portsmouth Waterway
West Sussex Waterways

MILITARY BOOKS
Battle over Portsmouth
Battle over Sussex 1940
Bombers over Sussex 1943-45
Bognor at War
Military Defence of West Sussex
Military Signals from the South Coast
Secret Sussex Resistance
Surrey Home Guard

OTHER RAILWAY BOOKS
Index to all Middleton Press stations
Industrial Railways of the South-East
South Eastern & Chatham Railways
London Chatham & Dover Railway
War on the Line (SR 1939-45)

BIOGRAPHY
Garraway Father & Son